WRITTEN COMMUNICATION

FOR

TODAY'S MANAGER

WRITTEN COMMUNICATION

FOR

TODAY'S MANAGER

Barbara Schindler Jones

Lebhar-Friedman Books
Chain Store Publishing Corp.
A Subsidiary of Lebhar-Friedman Inc.
New York

Library of Congress Cataloging in Publication Data

Jones, Barbara S   1921-
        Written communication for today's manager.

        Includes bibliographical references.
        1. Communication in management.   I. Title.
HF5718.J58   658.4'5   80-15315
ISBN 0-912016-87-6

Printed in the United States of America

5   4   3   2

Second Printing 1984

CONTENTS

INTRODUCTION

Chances are no manager would deny the importance of communication, whether it be used to keep the business functioning or to help him or her to cope with personal problems. On the job, the manager communicates with superiors, with colleagues, with subordinates, and with the public. Purposes for these communications vary from routine to dramatic; managers communicate to achieve results, to blow off steam, to buck for a promotion, to learn, to survive.

If writer Keith Davis is right, however, when he says "all [their] management acts must pass through the bottleneck of communication,"[1] the communication itself can be both a hindrance and a help, a bridge and a barrier. Even though they communicate constantly, managers cannot take the process or their understandings and skills for granted. Out of all possible messages and available information, what should be communicated? To whom? When? How? When should communication be in writing and when is it better to pick up the telephone or call a meeting? Once the manager has decided to put it in writing, how does he/she select the most effective medium, style, length, format? How can the message's impact be measured?

This book is designed to help with these and other concerns.

Although this book focuses on written communication, the reader needs to understand the impossibility of making any meaningful separation between written materials and the total context of organizational communication of which they are a part. Certain principles apply to communication senders and receivers, whether they be writers or speakers, readers or listeners. Because communication cannot occur in a vacuum, the real effectiveness of an inter-office memo cannot be understood without analyzing the problem that prompted it, as well as the whole tapestry of messages interwoven around it.

The memo involves not only words on paper but also reflects the climate of the organization and the quality of the relationships among people working together. Do people in the organization value communication and the efforts required to communicate well? Do people in the organization respect each other and each other's needs for clear and timely messages? Is the memo writer a credible source?

Written communication needs to be viewed not as a product but as a part of a total, dynamic, ongoing process. Although the memo may remain constant during the communication activities, the writer and the reader do not. And one communication begets another and that another.

This book is based on my notion that there is no such thing as a perfect communicator, but all of us can try to improve and learn to be more effective than we already are. *Written Communication for Today's Manager* is intended to be a combination of principles and practices, real retail examples and common sense. It will contain how-to's and even a few please-don'ts. The book is built on research in retail stores and upon my experience as a consultant and educator, working with individuals, groups, stores, and corporations.

Chapter 1 lays a foundation, outlining what goes on in the communication process generally, and specifically how written communication differs from oral. Next comes a discussion of why and when to write, some suggestions on how to get started, and a checklist of what successful writers do.

Chapters 2 and 3 deal with the specific problems of how to get and hold attention and how to personalize rather than generalize what we write. The overriding importance of establishing and clarifying a purpose for all written materials is the subject of Chapter 4. Chapter 5 deals with gathering and using information, while Chapter 6 explains the goals and processes of organizing ideas and supporting materials into meaningful patterns.

Language and meaning, as well as the difficulties in making abstract terms clear, and the problems of jargon and grammar, are among the subjects of Chapter 7. Chapter 8 is devoted to readability—what it is, how to measure it, and how to edit your material to achieve it. Chapters 9 and 10 look closely at specific forms of writing, beginning with reports, and moving on to other forms such as letters, memos, brochures and newsletters. Discussion questions, exercises, and case studies make up the Appendix.

Writing well comes from practice and from evaluating results. Did that memorandum clear up the problem? Did that manual eliminate time-consuming, costly mistakes? This book will be a more useful tool if the reader will not only read but also try the exercises and, as much as possible, put the content and procedural suggestions into practice in day-to-day retail managing.

Learning to write well takes time, patience, and work. It may mean breaking away from a comforting, habitual way of expressing yourself and trying new, simpler, and unfamiliar ways. Yet the task seems easier when you recall instances in which a sincere and friendly letter won a million dollars in business or good will, or a clear, problem-solving and timely report saved a business from losing a million dollars. Such writing is worth every bit of thought, care, and imagination the writer can manage.

—BSJ

Note

[1]Keith Davis, *Human Behavior at Work,* 5th ed. (New York: McGraw-Hill Book Company, 1977), p. 385.

WRITTEN COMMUNICATION

FOR

TODAY'S MANAGER

1

WRITTEN COMMUNICATION

What and how do writers communicate?

All our lives we are surrounded by communication signs, symbols, acts, and transactions. Messages abound. And because giving and getting information is such an integral part of our environment, we seldom take time to wonder what actually happens.

Definitions

Since we are dealing with the written form of communication, a logical starting place is with the definition of both terms, communication and written communication. A very broad, but useful, definition of communication as a whole is *all the procedures by which one mind affects another*. Other definitions point to the *exchange* or *sharing* of information and also to the *meeting of minds to achieve shared meanings*. Of course, the complete meaning of these definitions will develop throughout the book.

Written communication, in the context of this book, refers to all forms, formats, and purposes of the written word as it is used in managing people and retail businesses. Letters, memos, and reports are the most common forms but other kinds of written communication will be included where relevant.

Communication Is a Process

Suppose you are the assistant manager of a food store and need to give instructions to a stocker. You find the person and say, "Bob, do the milk, will you?" You are about to walk away when Bob, who is new to the job, asks, "Okay, but does that mean butter and eggs, too?"

This would be a puzzling conversation to someone who doesn't understand food store lingo. ("Doing the milk" in this case means restocking the dairy case.) Bob was wise to try to clarify the message before acting on it.

But let's look more closely at this simple communication transaction. You as the assistant manager were the *source* who *transmitted* the message to Bob, who was the *receiver*. Many messages stop there. But Bob added a vital ingredient, *feedback*, to indicate he didn't totally understand. The question Bob asked enabled you to adjust your message by telling him, yes, indeed, butter and eggs also needed stocking.

Feedback is what turns a one-way communication into a two-way, reciprocal process. Feedback is what happens as a result of the communication and is the primary way we have of checking to see if the message has been understood.

Further, feedback acts as a corrective mechanism the way the thermostat "tells" the furnace to go on or off, and the way the vane brings a windmill into the prevailing wind. Without feedback, our communication is like a shot in the dark, where we aren't sure whether we hit the target or not. With feedback, we can correct or adjust and explain in more detail when it seems necessary.

If Bob had not asked his question but had gone ahead and stocked only the milk, it would probably have been several hours before someone called the problem to your attention or you noticed the discrepancy between your intent and his actions. In this situation, you would probably eventually get feedback but it would come too late for you to change or clarify your original message.

Now let's suppose that as the assistant manager of our hypothetical store, you decided not to give oral instructions but to write out assignments for stockers and post them on a bulletin board. Opposite Bob's name you put "Milk." What are the chances that Bob will give you feedback that he's not sure whether he should do the butter and eggs? Chances are slim because now you are off in your office and cannot see Bob's puzzled expression. As a new employee, Bob may hesitate to come to your office and/ or interrupt if he sees you are busy. If you get feedback at all, once again it will be too late to clarify or correct your original message.

In such a situation, Bob would probably ask another stocker or clerk to explain if he saw that you were busy. But now the message is once-removed from the possibility of complete accuracy because the *feedback is secondhand,* having come from a source other than the original sender. The more people involved in clarifying other people's messages, the more possibility for error.

Differences Between Oral and Written Communication

The first of two main differences between speaking and writing continues our discussion of feedback.

1. Immediate versus delayed or nonexistent feedback.

When we write out information and mail or post it, we get feedback too late to make any changes or adaptations. What's worse, *we may never get any feedback at all*. Have you ever slaved over a complicated report and then waited for reactions from the people you sent it to? Sometimes you have a very long wait.

If you announce a special sale of vitamins with a newspaper display advertisement, you can tell something about the effectiveness of the ad by the number of people who buy that brand of vitamins that day or week. (But we must be careful not to assume that all customers came only because of the ad. Maybe some had already planned on getting vitamins; maybe some responded to colorful shelf arrangements, special packaging, or eye-catching posters or price tags.) But most written communication has even less direct cause-and-effect relationship than an ad.

By way of summary, feedback in response to written communication is very difficult both to get and to evaluate. But this doesn't mean you should ignore or undervalue the feedback you do get to your written communication. Even delayed feedback can help you do a better job on the next piece you write. Most important to remember is that tardy feedback is one major reason why writers should do the best job possible in the first place, making later adaptations and corrections less necessary.

2. Two different languages

Although English is what most of us speak and write, the oral and written versions are virtually two different languages. When we speak it is apt to be in short phrases, even snatches, and we may not complete our sentences. Pronouns may get widely separated from the word to which they refer but nobody cares because we clarify what we mean by tone of voice or a wave of the hand. Talking often comes out as colloquial, slangy, even profane.

But when we put words on paper, we follow a different set of rules. Written syntax and custom require that we complete sentences. In addition, the words and sentences are usually longer and more complex than we would comfortably say aloud. "Sure, Harry, okay," which sounds fine when spoken, becomes something like, "Herewith is our considered concurrence on this matter," when written. Manhole covers become "sewage access structure closure devices." Knowing that writing on a piece of

4

paper has more permanence than our spoken word, we are tempted to write in a formal, flowery style that sounds nothing like the way we talk.

True, there are occasions when formal and flowery writing is appropriate; when we are writing a tribute that will be formally presented to someone at a ceremony, for example. But usually our writing is more effective when direct and to the point. Careful writers know they can't afford to undermine their meaning by ambiguous pronouns or other grammatical lapses which would probably go unnoticed in spoken presentations.

Some teachers recommend that people "write the way they talk," and then are dismayed when the student turns in a rambling, disconnected discourse arranged in awkward clumps. Similarly, some speakers feel the only way they can control stage fright is to write out their speeches and read them to an audience. Unfortunately, what happens then is that the "speech" becomes an essay on its hind legs and the material lacks the spontaneity and directness of true speech.

Although understanding what happens in the communication process will help both writers and speakers improve, skill in one area may not transfer to the other. That's why an excellent conversationalist may be a dull writer and a skilled writer may be an uninspiring lecturer.

To summarize this point, we need to remember that written and oral communication are two different languages. Instead of trying to write as we talk, we should write in as clear, precise, complete, and forthright a manner as we can develop, while following commonly accepted rules of usage. Chapter 7 will have more to say about some grammatical and usage pitfalls to avoid.

Writing Versus Talking

One chain's district office has a slogan printed along the side of its memo pads, "GET IT RIGHT IN WRITING!" This may or may not be good advice. If the pronouncement is based on the notion that people are more apt to think through an idea before they write it, in contrast to "speaking off the tops of their heads," the slogan might encourage more careful communication. But if the slogan writer assumes that writing achieves more accurate results than speaking, he or she does not understand that face-to-face communication—which includes both nonverbal and verbal messages, as well as *instantaneous* feedback—is almost always the more accurate means of communicating.

But before you throw away all your memo pads and letterheads, let's look at the virtues as well as the liabilities of written communication.

When Is the Written Form a Wise Choice?

Too often, managers choose to write because they find it quicker and easier *for them* or because they can't break the memo-writing habit. Writing something can provide a satisfying catharsis, an opportunity to get something off our chests. But if this is the sole purpose, better leave the material in a drawer and reread it later rather than send it in the heat of anger or frustration.

Even if writing a memo is the easiest way for you to communicate, you need to back off and evaluate *results*. Ease for you should be balanced against your purpose, your subject matter, and the needs and concerns of your reader. A short cut for you could well be a time-consuming waste in the long run.

You should write instead of calling, going to see a person, or convening a meeting when:

1. **The material is too complex to be grasped or retained when presented orally.** As we all know, listening is hard work and memories can have a way of faltering. So if the ideas are many and involved, we will be better able to make sure they are received and retained, if we write them rather than speak them.

2. **You want to reduce the chances of being misquoted.** Having your words changed or taken out of context can readily

6

happen if you are speaking to an individual or a group because people often hear what they want to or expect to hear instead of what was actually said. This explains why officials usually hand out written statements about important issues at the beginning of press conferences. The written statement can be expanded upon or clarified orally, but the statement contains the essence in specific, unequivocal terms.

3. You want a well-thought-out reply. Even if your subject is short and simple, a memo will enable the reader to reread and think about the points you raise before responding. The quality of the reply, therefore, should be better than a quick spoken response.

4. You want to complete a message without interruption. In instances where you have thought about a problem in depth, marshalled your facts, and planned how to organize the material, interruptions and the chances of being sidetracked into irrelevancies can be more time consuming than beneficial. Putting it all in writing when the ideas are "hot" can turn out a better product.

5. You want a record. Because oral conversations or reports leave no trails behind them, they are difficult to verify. But the written word survives as a record of decisions or commitments.

6. You want to provide a reference. Similar to but somewhat different from having a record is providing a reference and a reminder for you and the readers of what has happened or perhaps that more needs to be done and/or communicated.

7. You want to reach several people with the same message in the same way at the same time. A quick announcement or memo to multiple readership ensures that all concerned "get the word." What's more, they get the *same* word. Timing is also important because people resent being the last to know, and people first to know sometimes have an unwarranted advantage.

8. It's cheaper. Management experts have computed the cost of producing a typical business letter. No matter how large or small the firm, the dollar amount is always astonishingly high because in addition to the material costs of stationery and postage, the calculations include the time spent by both management and clerical personnel. Nevertheless, the written form often turns out

7

to be less expensive than long-distance telephone calls or paying travel expenses to gather people together.

9. You want to avoid seeing someone. There could be a host of reasons, both professional and personal, why you might want to avoid a face-to-face confrontation at the time. Writing works best in this circumstance—as long as you use it as a temporary and occasional expedient and avoid making it a habit.

10. You prefer one-way communication. We have already stressed the importance of two-way communication and giving and getting feedback. But there are times, perhaps when a subject is routine or being closed, that you really don't need or want a reply.

11. You can't reach the person by telephone or in person. If you find the potential receiver of your message unavailable or you have to be out of the office when the person could return your call, the written form may be the best (or even the only) way to make contact.

Before deciding whether to write or use some other method, think first about the recipients of your communication. What would be the most effective (including *cost*-effective) means of getting through to them?

Getting Started

As all writers (including this one) can attest, there is something formidable about a blank piece of paper. Getting started, putting down those first faltering, inadequate words creates anguish and self-doubt. Good writing takes planning, thought, time, self-confidence, and work. Logical and disciplined communication requires a logical and disciplined mind. Effective writers always spend more time thinking and planning than they do writing.

Before they put anything but notes on that blank piece of paper, effective writers do five things:

1. Determine the purpose or purposes

Before doing anything else, good writers decide on a purpose. We only communicate when we want something to happen, when we want other people to do, think, or feel something *as a result of our communication*. *Why* are you writing? Unless you can answer that question in depth, you have no basis upon which to make such decisions as what to say, or how best to say or arrange it. Because understanding the need for and acquiring the ability to develop a clear purpose are so important, an entire chapter, Chapter 4, is devoted to the role of purpose in writing.

2. Analyze the audience

Next, good writers identify their reader or readers and try to learn as much about them as possible. Writing to everyone in a broadside approach seldom communicates what the writer intends. All writing should be directed to *someone*; not a vague someone, but a specific person or identifiable persons. Never a "mass" proposition, communication is always and ultimately a problem of getting an idea from one head to one head. Does the message need to go to one store, a group of stores, or all stores? Should the information go only to department heads or also to other employees? Who, precisely, are the people who will read the material? See Chapter 3 for more help in this area.

3. Acquire, analyze information

If you write a simple memo to confirm an understanding, you already have the necesary information in your head. The bulk of business writing, however, comes not in simple memos but in bulletins, newsletters, reports, and manuals that usually run on for more than a few sentences. For most managerial writing, it would be impossible (and pointless) to try to remember all the facts, figures, and references. You need to talk to people, look things up and pull together a variety of ideas *before* you start to write. Some people try to skip this preparation and planning phase and find themselves writing in circles and ultimately wasting time and energy. Chapter 5 gives suggestions on how to improve the gathering and analyzing of material.

4. Choose the medium and the format

Most organizations and stores have certain routine ways of communicating about certain problems. If head office personnel learn that the expected shipment of garden tools has been delayed and so will not be delivered in time for the projected promotion, a "flash" bulletin is the customary medium by which store managers are alerted that the sale must be postponed. "Flash" or "urgent" are printed in large letters across the top; perhaps the paper is color coded for different types of problems; perhaps the bulletin is numbered so that readers can tell if they are missing any in a sequence. Without habitual procedure to rely on, however, writers need to select a medium that best accomplishes the purpose for the specified readers. Write a letter? Routine memo?

After deciding on the best medium, consider next the form or format or physical appearance of the finished product. What would be the most effective size, shape, length? How should the material be arranged on the page? Type size, margins and white space, bindings, and other aspects are important details because they contribute to the success or failure of the message. A variety of media are compared and evaluated in Chapter 10; formats are discussed in Chapters 2, 6, and 9.

5. Organize, outline information

Poor writers just start writing and put down ideas as they occur to them. A workable technique for novelists, perhaps, but managers would do better to select an organization pattern to help the reader make sense of the information and understand the writer's frame of reference. Since grasping key ideas already taxes readers, they need all the help the writer can give them. Organization patterns make the reading and understanding easier. Outlining makes the writing easier. See Chapter 6 for more out organization.

Finishing the Job

Now that you have completed the five steps in planning and preparation, you are ready to do the actual writing.

6. First draft

For important and complex material, a first draft is a necessity. If you try to polish as you go, you find yourself bogged down and endlessly reworking the same sentence or paragraph. Effective writers get the essence down first, and polish separately.

7. Put aside; reread later

Unless the deadline is yesterday, allow enough time to put the first draft in a drawer and forget about it. Amazingly, the material will look different and your attitudes may have changed when you get out the pages and look at them later. This is the time to check for word choice and readability by doing your best to read from the reader's (not your) perspective. See Chapter 7 on language and meaning and Chapter 8 on readability.

8. Edit, rewrite

As better ways to phrase ideas and organize sentences and paragraphs occur to you, editing and rewriting naturally follow.

Not all writing needs editing and rewriting, of course. Perhaps you were lucky and skilled enough to turn out a polished draft the first time. But for most of us, anything over a page will require a second, even a third or fourth draft. Among the purposes for rewriting are to clarify and expand, but you also need to add interest and originality. While editing you can add that color and flair that are uniquely your style. See Chapter 8 for more about the editing process.

Summary

The better you understand the communication process and how written and oral messages differ, the better writer you can become. Under certain business circumstances, there are distinct advantages to the written or visual media. Suggested guideposts cover five steps to help the writer get started in planning and preparation and three steps to help with the actual writing.

2

ATTENTION

Why should I read it?

Sad, but true, the world teems with poor readers and even non-readers. People skip over, skim, and studiously ignore the printed word. Rarely do they give what we have written the full attention it deserves. Why is this? Among many possible reasons, three stand out:

Competition for time

Too much material has to be read. No thought or activity goes on without a piece of paper to guide it. Every manager knows the feeling of being inundated by a paper blizzard. Some days you are tempted to shovel it all out the door and forget it. But, of course, if you tried that, you would be the next item shoved out the door.

Growing demands of complex society

A recent report on adult illiteracy for the Ford Foundation pointed out that 23 million American adults have serious reading problems and in nine states more than half the adult population have not completed high school. According to the report, the reading and writing gap is widening. Moreover, skills once considered good enough for an American to function adequately are no longer sufficient in today's increasingly technological and complex world.

Picture orientation

Largely because of television and the movies, Americans do more passive looking than active reading. They have been conditioned to expect the message to come to *them* with little or no effort on their part. So if the printing looks long and complex, the potential reader will probably equate the reading with hard work and view it with distaste.

Attention Is Vital

Even well-written material will fail to inform, influence, or persuade if the reader's mind attends to something else. A school for advertising copywriters emphasizes the following slogan: *Remember, they don't want to read it!* All writers should have that slogan in mind every time they start to write. Busy, harassed people really don't want to read unless they have to, unless the material reaches out and grabs them. Readers can defeat writers right off the bat by taking away what writers must have—attention.

Managing means managing time and information. Since you don't have time to read every word of every message, you have learned to identify the material you don't have to read (now or at all) and also the kinds that can be skimmed or stashed away for later careful reading. Picturing the stacks of paper on your own desk can make you a more effective writer because you will learn to be brief and to the point and you will understand the need to catch and hold the reader's attention.

Deciding what (or whether) to read

Let's picture you arriving back at your desk after a three-day absence. In a hodgepodge pile are letters, reports, magazines, advertisements, memos, and bulletins. You pick up the piece of paper, which happens to be a letter, from the top of the pile. How do you decide whether to read it now, throw it away, or put it in the "read later" stack? Most people quickly analyze four basic factors before making that decision.

1. First impression. At a glance, you take in the overall appearance of the page. Is the material short or long? Does it have an attention-getting opener? Does it have eye appeal? Does it look interesting?

2. Relevance to the reader. Next, you look for the key idea and try to figure out what it has to do with you. You ask yourself, "Do I *need* to read it? Will it make me smarter, happier? Will it give me a change of pace in a pressure-packed day? What's in it for me?"

3. Purpose. Most readers will then try to determine the author's purpose, asking themselves such questions as, "Why was this written? Why was this sent to me? What is expected of me—is this memo straight information or does it mean I will have to do something?"

4. Author. "Who wrote this?" is another question the reader's preliminary glance tries to detect. "Do I know him or her? Is it somebody important or influential? Is it somebody with credibility? Or is it a form letter with a stock agency or department identification rather than an individual?"

If the answers to these four factors are both positive and readily apparent, you now make one last decision: read it now or later? Sometimes managers immediately plow through every sentence on all pieces of paper out of a sense of duty. But efficient time management calls for a now-or-later decision based on such aspects as urgency of the problem, how the written matter relates to individual and organizational goals, personal priorities, interest level, and the work involved. Sometimes readers make this decision on mood or whim. (And that's not necessarily always bad.) But fundamentally, *you don't want to read that letter.* The telephone is ringing, someone is waiting to see you, and you're expected at a meeting in twenty minutes. If that letter gets read now or ever depends upon its attention-getting value.

Consistently producing material that successfully catches and holds attention is an art, but one that can be learned. Showmanship and a sense of the dramatic are definite assets, as are knowing the reader and what approaches work best for him or her. Writers do not get and hold attention by writing in the same old way or by relying on tired, overworked phrases.

How to Get and Hold Attention

How do we go about breaking through the barriers of inertia and indifference? How do we attract favorable attention to our words and ideas? Let's look at five key pointers: the *opening, closing, purpose, relevance to the reader,* and *general appearance.*

1. Opening

Like a newspaper headline, the opening's function is to stop people—to stop them from moving on to something else. Readers are won or lost on the basis of openings alone. The *New Yorker* Magazine has a continuing feature titled, "Letters I Never Finished Reading," for which readers send in examples of openings that are illogical, inept or inane.

If the opening is interesting, the reader will assume the rest must be interesting and he or she will continue to read. But if the opening is muddled or unclear, or wastes time with unnecessary, rambling introductory material, or in some way insults or irritates the reader, he or she will start skimming, or worse, move on to the next piece of paper.

But openings that are merely "stoppers," perhaps relying on a gimmick or anecdote, are not effective either. The opening needs an *idea* that leads to the main subject. Phony attention-getters, in other words, turn the reader off. (Recently, an advertising pitch letter that caused me to stop reading began: "Dear Friend: I'm not joking. This is *not* an ordinary letter.")

Too many managers have a stock opening for letters that they use over and over. Typically, this acknowledges receipt of a previous letter or request by date, and doesn't tell the reader anything he or she didn't already know. Compare these two examples:

> **A.** Your letter of August 3rd has been received and your request for additional information duly noted. We are pleased to be able to supply you with the following
> . . .
> **B.** In answer to your question . . .

Rudolf Flesch calls the round-about opening a "false start" and says:

> Ninety-nine out of a hundred business letters start with an acknowledgement of the addressee's last letter. Have you ever asked yourself why? The only plausible answer I found is that it's always been done that way. It's an old, old custom.[1]

Let's look at some more interesting and effective attention-getting kinds of openers.

Start with a question. Some successful openers start with a question. Others start with a question that is then quickly answered. Here are two examples:

    A. When was the last time you stepped back and took a good look at the quality of writing done by you and your subordinates?

    B. Who is the real boss of our company? That's right, it's the customer.

Start with a zinger. Another effective opening statement is the one that is provocative, even startling, like the following:

    A. It's safe to say that the most productive writers, pound for pound, are not the professional literateurs but professional executives.

    B. Some food stores are managed today as if they still used horse-drawn delivery trucks.

Start with the main point or conclusion. Busy people appreciate the writer getting down to business instead of hemming and hawing. Here is a sample of a main point which the writer starts with and then develops in the body of the material:

    As you know, it is our policy not to allow salesmen to sell displays to any of our stores without prior authorization by bulletin from this office. Please review this policy with your Department Managers.

    The reasons this policy needs to be reviewed and reinforced are . . .

Start with an incident or story. Case histories, incidents, and illustrative stories can be good openers provided they are not too involved and are directly related to the main point. Here is an example:

    Recently, the district office received a letter from a customer who described how he and his wife were treated when they tried to return an unsatisfactory article to the store. The man began by saying, "We were prepared to lambaste the manager or whoever we could find."

Start with a hypothetical question or situation. Another way to stimulate the reader's curiosity is to open with a "what if" situation, such as:

Suppose you observed one of your employees putting merchandise in his pocket. What would you do?

2. Closing

Some writing seems to peter out instead of ending or concluding, as if the writer ran out of things to say and just stopped. Yet having a strong ending is second in importance only to having an attention-getting opening. The reader's interest is highest at the beginning and at the end (and some readers habitually skip over the middle entirely) so writers cannot afford to waste the high attention value of the closing. The closing should be the clincher, the reinforcement, the summary, the bringing together of the material's essence. Avoid endings that leave too much unresolved, dilute your main point, close on the wrong note or end weakly, without impact.

Some of the techniques suggested for openings can also be effectively used for closings, depending, of course, upon the purpose of the material or the specific response you want from your reader. Ending with a question, for example, would be appropriate if the request is simple, such as the following:

We have arranged for the next planning meeting to be held on Wednesday at 2 p.m. Can you come then?

Perhaps the most often used type of closing, particularly if the letter or report is longer than a few paragraphs, is the summary, in which the writer stresses the main points and objectives and wraps them into a coherent whole. When writing such a closing, ask yourself this: Even if my reader doesn't understand or skips over part of this report, *what is the key idea I want to make certain he or she gets?* What thought, above all else, do I want to leave in the reader's mind? The answers to these questions indicate what should be included in your summary type of closing.

3. Purpose

Have you ever read a three-page, single-spaced letter clear through without being able to figure out what the writer wanted you to do, think, or feel? Perhaps you found a clue in the last paragraph which then made it necessary for you to go back and reread the whole letter from a completely different frame of reference.

Writers have a way of burying their purpose within the verbiage or perhaps thinking that the "subject" at the top of the page takes care of the purpose too. Those writers who play a kind of "Guess what I'm thinking" game find their readers are not intrigued by the game and stop reading. Chances are high that the readers will not carry out the intention the writer had in mind because *they don't know what it is*.

Chapter 4 will go into this subject in depth. For now, let's emphasize the relationship between getting and holding attention and the reader's understanding of what the writer had in mind. Readers will lose interest unless the purpose is made clear and made clear early in the material.

4. Relevance to reader

"Why *me?*" is another question the reader wants answered immediately before he or she will give sustained attention to the material. Yes, Janet can tell at a glance that the pages in her hand describe a personnel problem in one of the stores. But Janet has no responsibility for personnel matters, and therefore resents having to waste valuable time trying to determine why the report was sent to her. Is it for information only? Then the report holds only peripheral interest for her and that will influence the way she reads. Is her job in some way affected? She shouldn't have to puzzle over this possibility.

Good written material quickly gets through to the self-interest of the reader. "What's in it for the reader if he or she reads?" is a question that should be answered early. There should be no doubt in the reader's mind about what the information has to do with her or him.

5. General appearance

Without looking at individual words, the reader gets an impression about the material from just the way it looks on the page. Interest will be created by an appearance of organization, balance, variety, and neatness.

In-house memos and bulletins can be forgiven incompleteness or sketchiness because they are communication within the family. But even here, the writer should be aware of the impression made by the appearance and should make certain the impression is what the writer intends.

For external letters and reports going outside the store or chain, such matters as quality of paper, attractiveness of letterhead, and how the typing looks on the page have vital importance. They may sound like picky subjects but the writer should never forget that all these aspects communicate. If the physical qualities of the letter or report lack appeal, the printed matter may never get read.

If the report is neatly and correctly typed, if balanced margins and adequate white space are used, if there are charts and graphs to project visual messages at a glance, the report is much more likely to be read. Appearances *do* count.

Compare Examples 1 and 2 on pages 22 and 23. Which one would be read first? Which one appears easier to read and understand?

XXXXX XX, XXXX

XX: XXXXXX XXXXXXXXXX

XXXX: XXXXXXXXXX   XXXX

XXXXXX: XXXXX XX XXXXXXXXXXXXXXX

XXXXXXXXXXXXXXXXXXXXXXXXXXXXXXXXXXXXXXXXXXXXXXXXXX
XXXXXXXXXXXXXXXXXXXXXXXXXXXXXXXXXXXXXXXXXXXX
XXXXXXXXXXXXXXXXXXXXXXXXXXXXXXXXXX
XXXXXXXXXXXXXXXXXXXXXXXXXXXXXXXXXXXXXXXXXXXXXXXX
XXXXXXXXXXXXXXXXXXXXXXXXXXXXXXXXXXXXXXXXXXXXXXXXXXXX
XXXXXXXXXXXXXXXXXXXXXXXXXXXXXXXXXXXXXXXXXXXX
XXXXXXXXXXXXXXXXXXXXXXXXXXXXXXXXXXXX
XXXXXXXXXXXXXXXXXXXXXXXXXXXXXXXXXXXXXXX
XXXXXXXXXXXXXXXXXXXXXXXXXXXXXXXXXXXXXXXXXX
XXXXXXXXXXXXXXXXXXXXXXXXXXXXXXXXXXXXXXXXXXXXXX
XXXXXXXXXXXXXXXXXXXXXXXXXXXXXXXXXXXXXXXXXXXXXXX
XXXXXXXXXXXXXXXXXXXXXXXXXXXXXXXXXXXXXXXXXXXXXXX
XXXXXXXXXXXXXXXXXXXXXXXXXXXXXXXXXXXXXXXXXX
XXXXXXXXXXXXXXXXXXXXXXXXXXXXXXXXXXXXXXXXXXXXXXXXXXXXXXXX
XXXXXXXXXXXXXXXXXXXXXXXXXXXXXXXXXXXXXXXXXX
XXXXXXXXXXXXXXXXXXXXXXXXXXXXXXXXXXXXXXXXXXXXXXXXXX
XXXXXXXXXXXXXXXXXXXXXXXXXXXXXXXXXXXXXXXXXXXXXX
XXXXXXXXXXXXXXXXXXXXXXXXXXXXXXXXXXXXXXXXXXXXXXXXX
XXXXXXXXXXXXXXXXXXXXXXXXXXXXXXXXXXXXXXXXXXXXX
XXXXXXXXXXXXXXXXXXXXXXXXXXXXXXXXXXXXXXXXXX
XXXXXXXXXXXXXXXXXXXXXXXXXXXXXXXXXXXXXXXXXXXXXX
XXXXXXXXXXXXXXXXXXXXXXXXXXXXXXXXXXXXXXXXXXXX
XXXXXXXXXXXXXXXXXXXXXXXXXXXXXXXXXXXXXXXX
XXXXXXXXXXXXXXXXXXXXXXXXXXXXXXXXXXXXXXXXXXXXX
XXXXXXXXXXXXXXXXXXXXXXXXXXXXXXXXXXXXXXXXXXXXXX
XXXXXXXXXXXXXXXXXXXXXXXXXXXXXXXXXXXXXXXXXX

Example 1.

Attention

XXXX xx, XXXX

XX: XXXXX XXXXXXXXXX

XXXX: XXXXXXX XXXX

XXXXXX: XXXX XX XXXXXXXXXXXXXXXXXXXXX

<u>XXXXXXXXXXXX</u>

XXXXXXXXXXXXXXXXXXXXXXXXXXXXXXXXXXXXXXXXXXXXXXXXXXXXXXXXXXXXXXX
XXXXXXXXXXXXXXXXXXXXXXXXXXXXXXXXXXXXXXXXXXXXXXXX
XXXXXXXXXXXXXXXXXXXXXXXXXXXXXXXXXXXXXXXXXXXXXXXXXXXXXX

     x.   XXXXXXXXXXXXXXXXXXXXXXXXXXXXXXXXXXXXXXXXXXXX

     x.   XXXXXXXXXXXXXXXXXXXXXXXXXXXXXXXXXXXXXXXXXXXXXXXXXX

     x.   XXXXXXXXXXXXXXXXXXXXXXXXXXXXXXXXXXXXXXXXXX

     <u>XXXXXXXXXXXXXXXXXX</u>

     XXXXXXXXXXXXXXXXXXXXXXXXXXXXXXXXXXXXXXXXXXXXXXXXXXXXXX
XXXXXXXXXXXXXXXXXXXXXXXXXXXXXXXXXXXXXXXXXXXXXXXX
XXXXXXXXXXXXXXXXXXXXXXXXXXXX

     XXXXXXXXXXXXXXXXXXXXXXXXXXXXXXXXXXXXXXXXXXXXX
XXXXXXXXXXXXXXXXXXXXXXXXXXXXXXXXXXXXXXXXXXXXXXXXXXXXXXXXX

     XXXXXXXXXXXXX

     <u>XXXXXXX</u>

     XXXXXXXXXXXXXXXXXXXXXXXXXXXXXXXXXXXXXXXXXX
XXXXXXXXXXXXXXXXXXXXXXXXXXXXXXXXXXXXXXXXXXXXXXXXXXX
XXXXXXXXXXXXXXXXXXXXXXXXXXXXXXXXXX

     XXXXXXXXXXXXXXXXXXXXXXXXXXXXXXXXXXXXXXX

     x.   XXXXXXXXXXXXXXXXXXXXXXX

     x.   XXXXXXXXXXXXXXXXXXXXXXXXX
XXXXXXXXXXXXXXXXXXXXXXXXXXXXXXXXXXXXXXXXXXXXXXXXXXXXXXXXXXXXXXXXX
XXXXXXXXXXXXXXXXXXXXXXXXXXXXXXXXXXXXXXXXXX

Example 2.

Summary

Working hard at sentence structure and making ideas march forward, as important as they are, contribute nothing if you do not gain the reader's interest and attention. Readers quickly determine what, when, and how to read. Such factors as the opening, closing, purpose, relevance to the reader, and general appearance are critical in getting and holding attention.

Note

[1]Rudolf Flesch, *The Art of Readable Writing* (New York: Harper & Row, Publishers, 1949), p. 46.

3

PERSONALIZATION

Do you mean me?

The previous chapter dealt with the importance of getting and holding attention without once referring to the best way of all: seeing that your writing emphasizes and spotlights the reader. Tailoring the message to fit the recipient ensures attention. "Why, this letter is obviously for and about *me!*" the pleased reader will note and then proceed to read with great care and concentration.

Too many business letters sound as if they could have been written by anyone and were intended to be read by anyone. They are impersonal, routine, and cold; stranger writing to stranger; machine to machine; or else they contain so much verbiage they appear to be written to impress rather than express. What a pleasant feeling to receive a letter that seems to have some thought behind it for the *person* who will read it.

Each of us humans is the center of his or her own world and for all but the most selfless, our self-interest means that we like to read about ourselves and we like to read material that is directed to us, as individuals, not us as a faceless group. Yet when we shift from the role of reader to that of writer, we continue to allow our self-interest to come first. This means we write more to ourselves than to the reader.

Store Manager Paul has a problem he wants to explain to the district manager. Without stopping to think about it, Paul will probably describe the problem from his own standpoint and outline what he has done and what he recommends. Unfortunately for Paul, the district manager is more concerned about the problem from *his* or *her* perspective (not Paul's) and wants to know what significance and relevance the problem has for her or him.

Henry Ford once said that the secret of success was being able to see the problem from the other person's viewpoint. This also applies to writing successfully. We should always be reader-conscious and provide what the reader needs and wants to know as our first priority and then, as second priority, what we want to tell. Attention, readership, and persuasion all improve when the reader feels personally and directly addressed.

In addition to writing more for ourselves than for the reader, another pitfall comes from attempting to be objective and overly businesslike. We *should* be objective and businesslike, but not at the sacrifice of sounding human. Trying too hard for objectivity and logic causes dull writing and poor readership.

Personal Pronouns

Another reason for lack of personalization occurs when we try to avoid the use of personal pronouns. Because it sounds too subjective, and somehow immodest, to use "I," writers box themselves into awkward thought and clumsy composition. Substitutes for first-person pronouns, such as "The undersigned went to the head office," don't fool anyone about the identity of the writer or sound any less modest than "I went to the head office." Using the impersonal third person, such as "It is always appreciated when our charge customers pay their bills promptly," goes a long way around to avoid saying, "I appreciate your paying promptly." Of course, hiding behind third-person objectivity offers a way to keep from having to state your own position or opinion, which may be appropriate in some reports or policy statements but seldom in correspondence.

Some people compromise between using "I" and sounding impersonal by using "we." This sometimes works but "We feel you are doing a good job" looks strange if the boss is the only one who signs the letter, unless he or she explains who "we" are. "We" could mean you (the reader) and I (the writer) together, or all of us in the company. This kind of ambiguous writing caused Mark Twain to remark, "Only kings, editors, and people with tapeworm have the right to use the editorial we."

There are writers who seem to feel that using "myself" is better than "I." Yet, "Feel free to contact Harriet or myself," is awkward, and so is, "Both the boss and myself are planning to come to your store." Do you share the lurking suspicion that writers who use "myself" when they mean "I" or "me" are trying to cover their uncertainty about which is grammatically correct? (For the record, in the first example, the correct form would be "Feel free to contact Harriet or *me*," and in the second, it should be "Both the boss and *I* . . .")

Those writers who can't stand to use personal pronouns but who don't like substitutions either sometimes try to avoid pronouns altogether. Typical examples of this ploy are: "Was pleased to learn . . ."; "Wish to inform that . . ."; and "Sincerely regret to advise that . . ." Such language more properly belongs in telegrams, mailgrams, and cables which charge by the word.

Unless a company policy forbids you to use personal pronouns, by all means use them for directness and personalization. When you talk about your staff as "we" and yourself as "I" and other people involved as "they" you sound natural and human.

Although using "I" whenever appropriate is encouraged, the emphasis should be more on "you" than "I" in order to appeal to the reader's self-interest. Advertisers and sales personnel successfully use the "you" approach all the time. You never catch an advertiser writing that *he* wants to sell this product because *he* wants to make some money. Instead, he will write that *you* need this product and this is what it can do for *you*.

Analyzing the Reader or Readers

The better you know someone, the better you can communicate with her or him. If the person is well known to you, you have shared experiences upon which to draw and you can predict how that person will react to information presented in a certain way at a certain time.

When you sit down to write a personal letter to an old friend, for instance, you have an image of that person in your head and what you say and how you say it are automatically personalized. You go into sufficient detail to fill in the gaps in the friend's understanding of what you are writing about; similarly, you can take shortcuts in referring to subjects with which your friend is already familiar.

Obviously we can never know as much about strangers as we know about our friends. But we should try, nevertheless, to learn as much as possible about our readers in order to reach them effectively. What are some of the aspects it would be useful to know about our readers? Here is a partial list which you can expand to fit your specific readership analysis needs.

Age
Sex
Education
Occupation (title, where employed, how long, job duties)
Economic status
Basic motivations, objectives
Primary interests, beliefs, values
Knowledge of the subject
Attitudes about the subject
Attitudes about you, the writer

At this point, you are probably thinking, "Do I really need to know all that just to write a memo?" No. But the more you know, the better you can personalize your writing and keep it from sounding like mass-produced form letters. Naturally, you will weigh the importance of what you are writing before deciding how much time you can afford to spend on reader analysis. Simple, routine matters will probably require little. If there is a lot at stake, however, you can't afford *not* to spend time on analysis.

Who is to be written to is just as important as *what* is to be written. Managers need to select their audiences first because that determines *how* the message will be put together. Should this message go to a given unit or the whole store? Is the memo intended for certain positions (the bakery manager, the meat manager, or new employees) or certain units (personnel, training, or sales), or for certain designated individuals?

What happens if you're writing to several people at a time? For one thing, don't think of them as a group. Communication is never received by a group, only by individuals. Are the members of the mailing list sufficiently similar so that you can generalize and make one adaptation fit all? Sometimes you can generalize and make assumptions about the people you don't know well based on those you do. On other occasions it would be folly to make such assumptions. If, for example, you are attempting to persuade or convince the readers about an extremely important subject, then you would be better off to go to the extra effort of writing individual letters that can be truly personalized.

Adapting to the Reader

Just as when you write to a personal friend, you should write business letters to one person at a time. It helps to visualize the reader and write directly to that image. Whenever possible, use the reader's name; avoid impersonal salutations and sign-offs; refer to shared interests and experiences; use language that is meaningful to the reader; use a friendly, helpful tone; and wherever appropriate, use humor, a light touch, or an unusual turn of phrase.

Let's look at each of these suggestions in more depth.

1. Use names.

Thanks to computerized word-processing systems, even mass mailings can now include the addressee's name in the body of the letter as well as the salutation without skipping a beat. The fact that so many advertisers and sell-by-mail writers use this technique points up the importance of the use and repetition of a person's name. Using the reader's name in the body of the letter creates sure-fire personalization *unless* it has obviously been done by machine or is overdone to the point of sounding artificial or strained.

2. Avoid impersonal salutations and sign-offs.

Writers routinely address people and close their letters in impersonal, overworked ways, thereby losing important opportunities to personalize. Openers like "Dear Sir," "Dear Friend," or "Occupant" are not personalized; "Dear Tom," or "Dear Mrs. Thompson" are.

For years, lazy managers and secretaries have been using "Dear Sir," "Dear Madam," and "Gentlemen," to avoid having to look up a name. They might as well use "To Whom It May Concern." A little digging can usually unearth the name of the person you are writing so that he can be greeted as "Mr. Johnson," if you don't know him personally, or "Sam," if you do. But if it seems impossible to learn what the firm's advertising director's name is, then address him or her as "Dear Director," rather than fall back on tired old terms.

An important caution deserves attention here. Be sure that the title is sexless if you don't know the sex of the addressee. "Dear President" or "Dear Manager" are fine for either sex. But avoid titles like "Sales*man*" or "Fore*man*" unless you are certain the position is held by a man. (If you know that much then you ought to be able to learn the name.)

Above all, don't be guilty of the slipshod practice of using "Dear Sir" under an unmistakably feminine name. Machines can perhaps be forgiven for not knowing that mailing lists to people in traditionally masculine fields might include some women. But this irritating slip has even been known to occur when the letter was typed by a real live (but evidently unthinking) secretary.

Currently there is a movement away from using "Dear So and So" on business letters, and mercifully becoming extinct also, is "My dear Mrs. Ward." "Dear" hardly fits the boss or coworkers, let alone a stranger you have never met. An endearing term seems particularly inappropriate when the subject of the letter is a complaint or in a situation where the addressee is not at all dear to you. Salutations and closings aren't really necessary in in-house memos but something seems called for when the letter goes outside.

The To/From format, as well as the use of an Attention line, are two ways to avoid "Dear," as in the following examples:

To: Mary MacPhail
From: Jim Jordan
Subject: Annual Report
           (Body of the letter starts here without
               a salutation.)

To: Purchasing Department
           P&Q Stores
Attention: Mary MacPhail
From: Jim Jordan
Subject: Annual Report
           (Body of the letter starts here without
               a salutation.)

Somebody has suggested that letters should start something like "Salu Mr. Brown" or "Salu Ms. Cohen" instead of using

"Dear" because "Salu" is the root of words in a number of languages meaning "salutations" or "I salute you." Other substitutes for the endearment, "Dear" are "Good morning, John" (and if you're fussy about exactness, you wonder how John reacts if he opens the letter in the afternoon) and "Hello there, Lois" (which sounds too flippant for business correspondence). Evidently, we will continue to see "Dear" in use until someone comes up with an effective substitute that catches on.

Sign-offs offer another opportunity for personalizing. "Sincerely" survives as an all-purpose version that is almost always appropriate, whereas "Yours very truly" or "Very sincerely yours" sound flowery and somewhat ridiculous when you look at what they *mean*. Depending upon the circumstances and the relationship between writer and readers, "Cordially" or "Best wishes" or "Enjoy your day" offer refreshing changes from the routine.

If the writer falls into the trap of using the same closing for all letters, other attempts at personalization are negated. One manager, for example, likes the sound of "With kindest personal regards, I remain . . ." and uses it without variation. His readers (and certainly his secretary) must long for a change.

3. Refer to shared interests and experiences.

If you refer to a conversation between you and the reader, or recall some activity or experience the two of you shared, the reader knows he or she is being written to personally rather than routinely. These kinds of references get attention because they are unique and compelling.

In some consulting work done for a bank, I examined many letters written to clients of the trust department. As you know, trust officers work very closely with their customers and become almost like members of the family. Trust officers are frequently invited to dinner parties, weddings, and even funerals. Yet in the correspondence examined, I rarely found a personal reference. The letter writers seemed determined to perpetuate the stereotype of bankers as stodgy, stuffy, and distant.

Bankers are not the only ones who fail to make use of personal contacts to help personalize their letters. Think of the managers who routinely refer to past correspondence instead of noting past face-to-face encounters. "Thanks for taking time to meet me for lunch last week—and wasn't that shrimp excellent?" is a better bridge than a trite acknowledgment of a previous letter.

4. Use appropriate language.

Formal, stuffy language doesn't lend itself to personalization because it holds the reader at arm's length.

In order that our files show you have received the aforementioned items in the above-captioned account, please sign and return the copy of this letter in the envelope provided.

Such writing is unnatural and outdated. Even though personal pronouns are used, the letter sounds as if it were written to a nonperson. Personalization and more natural language (as well as ten fewer words) can be achieved by rewriting the sentence to read:

So we'll know you got the materials, please sign and return the copy of this letter in the enclosed envelope.

Your choice of language should reflect what you learned from analyzing your reader. You will not use a specialized vocabulary or jargon if your reader has a different orientation. You will not use "legalese" when writing to a nonlawyer. You will avoid abstractions when the meaning could be misinterpreted. You will not use literary or other allusions unless you know they will be fully understood or unless you explain them.

Some writers, when writing to less educated people, have a tendency to write down. They feel they must confine their writing to the simplest of words and the shortest of sentences in the first-grade-reader vein of "See Spot run." This insults the reader just as much as overblown, pompous writing does. Tailor your choice of language to the reader, yet with the recognition that all readers have some background of knowledge and experience, whether or not it came from formal education. Choose words that sound honest, natural, and straightforward, and you seldom go wrong.

5. Use a friendly, helpful tone.

Related to language choice is the overall effect, or tone, of your material. When we talk with someone, we can use nonverbal communication such as a smile or a humorous inflection to convey that our intent is friendly. Words on paper have to stand alone and we can never be sure what tone of voice our reader will "hear" in our writing. To help with this problem, we should avoid negative words and phrases like the following which seem to point a scolding finger at a naughty child.

> You *failed* to include the material promised.
> You *claim* you were not told about the meeting.

How do you sound? Friendly and helpful or busy and distant? Do notes of criticism, anger, or sarcasm come through? Pay attention to your "tone of voice" because it reveals a lot about you and your attitude toward the reader.

Contrast the following two letters written on the same subject. Both are personalized but note the difference in tone and warmth.

> Your handling of the details of my visit was appreciated. The meetings were useful and well organized.

> As always, it was fun to visit your area. I was particularly impressed by your recounting how your grandfather organized the first store in town.

Note also the difference in "objectivity" and being "businesslike ." The second writer was willing to share some of her or his feelings and, in so doing, sincerely complimented the reader.

Effective letter writers can put messages across—even bad news or unpleasant problems— in a friendly way, using words that are clear but do not put the reader down. The tone of the letter makes the difference. Where one letter irritates a person, another, which uses tact and consideration, will win compliance or cooperation. Business-letter writers cannot afford to forget that all readers of their letters are present or potential *friends of the company*. Would you scold or antagonize a friend? Even in the middle of a conflict or controversy, wouldn't you go a long way to give a friend the benefit of the doubt no matter how the situation appeared?

Approaching each letter in the spirit of friendliness, being positive, and wanting to help can improve both your tone and your personalization. Provide solutions instead of problems, put yourself out a bit, and your readers will begin to look forward to getting your letters.

6. Use humor and a light touch.

True, business matters are seldom funny, and trying to come up with jokes at the wrong time can backfire disastrously. But we don't always have to be deadly serious either. Writing about a humorous incident, particularly if the joke was on you, can be both disarming and a delightful attention-getter. Some people who are naturally witty and have a colorful way with words hesitate to use those skills in their business correspondence. What a shame! They could brighten their associates' day—and maybe even increase their sales volume.

Compare the following two letters from customers on the same subject. Which letter do you suppose got passed all around the store (and up to the district office) and which will be remembered longer?

Dear Manager:

We recently had to return a defective item to your store and we want you to know we appreciated the courtesy your clerk extended to us.

Sincerely,
A. Customer

Dear Mr. Baskins:

We weren't very happy when we had to make a special trip to your store to return that meat thermometer that didn't work. But the clerk who took care of us was so polite and nice and quick to apologize, we FORGOT to jump all over him. There's never anyone in your store to yell at! That's no fun. When I feel like taking out my frustrations on incompetents, I have to go somewhere else.

Sincerely,
Grateful Customer

Humor can often save the day and turn a messy problem into a good belly laugh, or a defeat into a triumph. An enterprising young man got the advertising copywriter job over many competitors because of a sense of humor. He had written in his letter of application that he had received a 100 percent response to a mailing piece he had prepared. When the interviewer asked to see the mailing piece, the young man replied, "You have the only copy in your hand."

Summary

Letters that capture attention, get read and acted upon, are those written by real people to be read by real people. Personalization depends upon analyzing the reader so the writer can adapt and tailor the information. Suggested adaptations include the use of personal names, selecting better salutations and closings, referring to shared interests and experiences, using appropriate language and a friendly tone, and finally, using humor and color.

4

PURPOSE

What do you want from me?

When you write to a friend, your only purpose may be to make contact or to share a piece of news. You don't trouble with analyzing your motives, you just sit down and write. But if you *did* analyze your inner feelings, you would find there was at least one basic urge or impulse that caused you to write to a particular friend at a particular time.

Maybe your silent thought processes went something like one or more of the following:

1. "That story in the newspaper reminded me of Marie and that silly scrape we got into when we were in high school. I think I'll write and tell her I was thinking of her."
2. "I really should write to Marie because I haven't answered her last letter and it came weeks ago. Not much has happened to me recently but I can at least drop her a short note."

3. "I'm pleased and excited about my promotion. Who can I share the good news with? I know, I'll write to Marie because she would want to know about it and she will be happy for me."

Before you write to Marie, you need a stimulus; it could be external (the newspaper article) or internal (an urge to share some news). But mixed up in your thinking and feeling about the possible letter are both *motives* and *purposes*.

Distinction Between Motive and Purpose

A *motive* is a personal benefit or satisfaction you expect to derive from writing; a *purpose*, on the other hand, is the response you hope to elicit from your reader.

Let's look at the previous three examples of thinking about writing a personal letter and try to sort out the possible motives and purposes.

Although making the distinction between motive and purpose may not be very important in personal correspondence, in business writing it is. It boils down to this: if you don't know where you're going, how do you know when you've arrived?

Example	*Possible Motive(s)*	*Possible Purpose(s)*	*Possible Hoped-for Response(s)*
1	Keep friendship alive.	Make contact; to entertain.	She will feel good about being remembered and hearing from me; she will write back to me.
2	Keep friendship alive; discharge obligation; get	Make contact; to inform.	She will understand that although I'm busy and don't have much news, I feel

38

Example	Possible Motive(s)	Possible Purpose(s)	Possible Hoped-for Response(s)
	rid of guilty feeling.		our friendship is important enough for me to take time to write; she will write back to me.
3	Brag about promotion; intensify and prolong feeling good about myself.	To inform; to share information.	She will understand the importance of the promotion to me; she will write her congratulations.

"*Why* am I writing this letter?" can be a creative but often overlooked question. Some managers mistakenly think their purpose is merely to write a letter or turn out a news release—but those are methods not purposes. Except in writing memos to ourselves, our writing always addresses readers and we are trying to inform or convince or delight them, explain something, or make them see or feel what we believe or have experienced.

To get at the specific purpose, we need to ask ourselves: What do I want the readers to do, think, or feel about this letter when or after they read it? True, our general goal is to get a message across to the right people in the most effective way. But then what? If nothing happens, or if you don't get the response you want, you have not achieved your purposes.

Now let's do a similar analysis of a business situation. To set the stage, let's say your store was one of the first in your area to experiment with the Universal Product Code. Coincidentally, you were asked to write brief reports on the code's effectiveness for (1) the district manager; (2) the local newspaper; and (3) the newsletter of a service club to which you belong. You gathered, organized, and presented similar information, but how might your motives and purposes differ in each case? Let's see.

Report Readers	*Motive(s)*	*Purpose(s)*
District Manager	Show how much information you have; enhance your standing with those higher up; help solve a problem.	To *inform* about how the system works in general and in your store; to *persuade* that the method be tried in other stores.
Newspaper readers in community	Get free publicity for your store; show the community your store is in the forefront of new technology; get your name before the public.	To *inform* readers about how the system works and the advantages to them; to *persuade* potential customers to come to the store to see the system in action.
Service club members and families	Show how much information you have; enhance your standing in the club, your community, and your organization; get free publicity for the store; get your name before the public.	To *explain* how the system works; to *inform* about its advantages and disadvantages; to *win* new customers for the store.

Because your purposes and readership vary, you deliberately organized and slanted your information differently for each report. You would certainly not write the reports or articles in the same way for all three audiences.

Remember that purpose has to do with the response you want from your reader. Literary writing is concerned with expressing oneself; but *business writing is concerned with influencing others*.

Some managers confuse their purpose with the subject about which they are writing. Listed at the top of the memo might be "Subject: Thanksgiving decorations," which seems very clear to the manager. But the *purpose* of the memo (which the readers had to figure out for themselves) was to make sure that the decorators were able to get into the store after hours.

Modern managers avoid confusing the reader by making certain that both the subject and the purpose of the letter are clear from the beginning. Both subject and purpose can be clarified in the first paragraph ("I am writing to you about this because . . .") or listed right at the top:

To: Store Manager
From: District Manager
Subject: Employee solicitation
Purpose: To explain how our employee solicitation policy
            conflicts with the NLRB ruling and what we
            must do about it.

Without the addition of the purpose statement, the reader has only a vague idea of what the letter is about and *no* idea of what it has to do with him or her.

So much time is saved when the person receiving the message knows its purpose. You can quickly respond if you see at once that the letter came to you because you will have the responsibility or authority to act, or because you will profit from having the information, or for other reasons. Spelled out reasons give the reader a vital and immediate frame of reference.

Unless you fully understand the purpose for writing, you cannot effectively choose between alternatives. How will you organize and develop the material? Is all the information you have relevant and necessary? Will you use a formal or informal style? What format would be best? These and other questions cannot be answered outside of a frame of reference and the writer's purpose provides that frame. The choices made along the way can be labeled wise or unwise only in relation to how well they helped the writer accomplish his or her purpose.

Four General Kinds of Purposes

Business writing usually has one or more of four general purposes. Of course, there may be secondary or related purposes, but almost always one major purpose predominates.

1. To get something

Usually what we want to get is *information* or data that we need for our decision-making. But also in this category would be ordering products or making requests for products or services. We want the reader to send or give us what we have asked for.

2. To give something

Once again, this is usually information. Examples include giving instructions, explaining the results of decisions, making announcements about new products or services or policy changes. Much business writing also confirms, validates, and agrees. You have only done part of the job, however, unless you make clear why you are giving the reader this information, what it has to do with him or her, and whether you expect an action or reaction.

3. To persuade or activate

In one sense, all business writing aims at selling (a product, a service, an idea, an image) but in this category we can put those purposes that are designed to convince people to do specific things for us. Some examples of persuasive purpose would be to try to get people to (a) buy your products or services (or to sell you theirs); (b) create a desire for your products or services; (c) help you solve a problem; (d) cooperate with you to change a policy or resolve a complaint; and (e) pay up an overdue account. In this type of writing, you want a specific action or change; you want the reader to make a commitment, and/or change an attitude or behavior.

4. To win friends

Although the purpose here is to get people to like us for the sake of furthering our business interests, this category differs from persuasion in that our writing does not aim at a specific action or result. Writing for this purpose usually takes place as part of a long-range campaign rather than a single effort, and includes all writing that attempts to create good will, improved public relations, or a favorable image. Material would generally be light, amusing, or entertaining. Examples are thank-you's, congratulations, or apologies, as well as other out-reach efforts to maintain or advance business relationships.

Expressing the Purpose

Occasionally, you should let your purpose come through by implication rather than by bluntly stating it. A subtle approach works best when your purpose is a delicate (let's hope not a devious) one. You wouldn't, for example, label your purpose when you are trying to soothe an irate customer or get a favorable outcome in a legal dispute. But even in these instances, when the purpose is not explicitly stated, the writer should have his or her purpose clearly in mind for the reasons already given.

When the purpose is to inform or persuade, being up-front about our hoped-for response usually pays dividends by saving the reader's time and keeping him or her from being confused. A general rule of thumb, also, relates to the length and formality of the writing: the longer and more complex the letter or report, the more necessary an early and explicit statement of purpose.

Summary

Poor writers begin writing without first thinking through the hoped-for result, or purpose, of what they are writing. Once writers know their specific purpose or purposes, they can make better choices about organization, format, style, and language. Business writing usually has one of four basic purposes: to get something, to give something, to persuade, or to win friends.

5

GATHERING INFORMATION

What do I need to know and where can I find it?

Writers seem to operate under one of two conditions—either they feel they have to say something or they have something to say. Of course, these two conditions are not always mutually exclusive and there is nothing inherently wrong in responding to the urge to communicate, in feeling that you *have* to write that letter. But there is no substitute for knowing what you are talking or writing about. Fiction writers can make up "far-out" fantasies, but business writers must deal with facts, figures, and down-to-earth, real information.

Sometimes the only information you need to write an intelligent letter already exists in your brain. Here your problem is to sift, sort out, and select. At other times, perhaps when you are responding to a query, you gather data from such common sources as the file cabinet and the last monthly report. Here your problem is in knowing where to look for what you need and how to pull it together.

A third and much more difficult situation occurs when you have to write about something for which there is no precedent and you have no files. What then? Where do you start? Beginning writers may respond as they did when they had to write a research paper in school—by charging off to the library. But the library may or may not be the best place to go looking, particularly in the early stages. More about that later.

If the boss asked for a report, before you go searching for information, you must first do some thinking and planning. Remember the advice to clarify your purpose in Chapter 4? With the boss's help, you need to determine why he has asked for the report. Will it attempt to solve a problem? Prove something? Next, you need to know who will read the report and do some reader analysis. Is the report for the boss alone or will it be passed along the chain, either up or down or laterally? Will it be shared with people outside the organization who may need special adaptations of scope or language? Review Chapter 3 for reader analysis and adaptation concepts.

As a "for instance," let's say that the report the boss wants focuses on electronic banking facilities in food stores. He has read or heard about experiments in a few stores around the country and he wants to know the answers to such questions as:

What kind of facilities are there?
What has been the experience of stores that have tried them?
Do most customers like and use them?
What are cost, space, and personnel requirements?
Would you recommend that your chain begin a pilot banking facility in one or more of its stores?

In your discussions with the boss, you have determined that he sees the purpose of your report as *to inform*, to supply data, with the possibility of persuasive elements added if your findings cause you to make a strong recommendation either for or against the pilot facility. You have also learned that the report's ultimate readership depends on both your findings and writing ability. "If the material you dig up is significant and if the report is well written," says the boss, "I'll buck it up to top management and see that you get credit for authorship. Otherwise, it will end up in my file, most likely the round file beside my desk."

So your purpose appears fairly clear and specific, but your readership has some variables. After some more thinking you decide to assume that your findings will be significant, that you will do a good job, and therefore you might as well plan from the beginning that top management, as well as your boss, will eventually read the report.

Only now are you ready for the *what, where,* and *how* of information gathering.

What Information Do You Need?

In our electronic banking example, the boss has simplified the answer to "what" by giving you some specific questions for which to find answers. He has also indicated that you should not limit your research to these questions and should feel free to present whatever information and data you feel are relevant. But proceed with caution. People who enjoy research and digging out interesting facts and ideas may have to use a tight rein on themselves to keep from galloping off in all directions. The best means of avoiding wasted effort when gathering material calls for the discipline of keeping your purpose constantly in mind and gathering *only information that serves the purpose*.

The information your report will supply will consist of *facts, opinions, inferences,* and *judgments*. Let's look at each of these in more detail.

Facts are phenomena that can be verified in some way. But since we can't all run around proving everything for ourselves, we have come to rely on other people's observations (within limits) and sources such as encyclopedias and atlases. Among the facts you will need for your report are the different kinds of banking facilities already in use, their cost, and typical space and personnel requirements.

47

Opinions are beliefs or conclusions that certain facts or ideas are probably true or likely to prove so. View them as tentative appraisals that may be changed when you acquire new or contradictory information. Among the opinions you will need for your report are expressions from store personnel and their customers who have tried the banking system. In addition, you may include your own opinions as part of your findings.

Inferences are interpretations or conclusions that go beyond the facts, from the known to the unknown. For example, when we see an approaching car with its signal light flashing, indicating a planned left turn, we make an inference that the car will turn left at the next corner. Experienced drivers recognize that their inference of what the car will do is based only on *probability*, not fact. The only fact involved is that the signal light is blinking. Guessing what the driver will actually do amounts to drawing inferences. Other possible inferences include (1) the driver forgot to turn off his signal light, (2) he is not aware that it is on, (3) it is a defective light, or (4) the driver really intends to turn left at a driveway that is a half block past the corner.

Although you will undoubtedly include inferences in your report, you will do your best to recognize them as such and not mix them up with facts. For instance, if you should interview a store manager who has instituted electronic banking, you may make note of the number of customers who used the facility in a given period (fact) but when the manager tells you that the facility increased his sales volume in that period, you are on more shaky (inferential) ground. It would be fallacious reasoning to assume that the additional customers or larger sales occurred *because* of the banking facilities. (This would be confusing causation with correlation.) If, on the other hand, the store manager has proof (perhaps through impartial customer surveys) that the banking facility actually brought more people into the store and therefore increased sales, then the information can be presented as fact.

Judgments are conclusions we make based on all the information (facts, opinions, and inferences) we have obtained. In your interviews you will hear judgments expressed and you, in turn, will make some based on your findings.

Wherever possible, effective reports separate facts, opinions, inferences, and judgments. Obviously, because the lines between are thin, separation isn't always possible.

Where Will You Find the Information You Need?

Depending on the complexity of the subject and information needed, one or all of the following can help.

1. An often overlooked source is *within the writer*. Before dealing with a particular subject, review your own knowledge and experience. Such reflection not only unearths a good source of evidence, but also provides a basis for determining the size of the gap between what you know and what you need to investigate.

2. Second, look at *materials already at hand*. Your own personal and professional libraries and files are often useful.

3. Third, you could *talk with friends and colleagues* and assess both their knowledge of the subject and their ability to lead you to other knowledgeable people or sources. In our electronic banking example, the boss should be asked for references he already knows about.

4. Other potential suppliers of information include *institutions* (such as banks and other financial organizations) and *experts* in the field or subject. From these avenues might come leads to oral materials (lectures, tapes, films, radio and television programs) and written materials (books, magazines, pamphlets).

5. Now you are ready to ask the *library* for help. Invaluable card catalogues and index guides save you wandering around unproductively. Don't overlook that wonderful person, the reference librarian, who can sometimes save you hours by giving you immediate answers or telling you where to look.

6. Also available are countless *special libraries*. Universities and colleges have specialized libraries, such as for business or law or engineering, and most large corporations have their own libraries and personnel to help the lay person. For our banking report example, you would certainly be wise to consult banking institutes and ask about their special libraries.

As mentioned earlier, trying to use the library too soon may only frustrate both the library user and the librarian. In large libraries, you could get lost for days just among the rooms and shelves labeled Banking, Finance, or Economics. Libraries are excellent sources for *specific* information and the place to go only after you have narrowed the subject and/or have a great deal of experience in knowing how best to use the library's extensive resources. For example, patrons have been known to ask for a "book on law" when all they really wanted to know was the location of the nearest Small Claims Court.

For our electronic banking report, the library (particularly a *special* library) could be most useful after you have explored the subject and have enough background to know what you don't know and which of multiple avenues you want to travel. Use the telephone first to save time and energy and by all means consult the reference staff.

How Can You Get the Information You Need?

Reading and listening are the two principal ways we gather information. Since random reading wastes time, you should have a plan and get help from some of the sources previously identified. Listening and conversing, such as in the process of an interview, can yield excellent results if skillfully done. Conversing with people about the subject under investigation can serve two purposes: not only can the discussion be the source of ideas but also an opportunity to test out your tentative thinking about the subject.

Going and seeing for yourself, as in making field trips and direct observations, also helps get information. For the banking report, you could write much more intelligently if you had personally seen the in-store electronic funds transfer system in action, both with automatic teller and with store personnel. If going in person is not possible or practical, you may still gather necessary information by telephone and by mail, using letters if the material is simple and survey forms or questionnaires for the more complex.

Two problems should concern us in how we gather information: *perception* and *objectivity*. Just as witnesses to the same traffic accident may provide conflicting testimony, so might your perceptions vary from other people's. Do you see only what you expect to see or want to see? And what about your biases and preconceived ideas about the subject under investigation? To be an effective investigative reporter, you need to build in one or more means of checking for accuracy, such as gathering information from a variety of people and institutions, and particularly from disinterested, neutral sources.

How to Keep Track of Information Gathered

For complex reports or letters, you may find the stack of materials growing to unmanageable proportions. Although styles and preferences vary and each person should develop her or his own organizational system, here are some starter suggestions.

1. Keep two sets of note cards, one as a bibliography of the sources used and the other for note-taking of the key ideas discovered in reading, interviewing or in other ways. Bibliography cards should contain such data as source and need dictate.

Here are some sample bibliography cards:

Book

Author or editor	Publisher
Title	Publication date
City of publication	Relevant page numbers

Abbot, Helen. <u>Modern Banking</u>. New York: American Banking Institute, 1978.

pp. 66-68 Electronic funds transfer

Article in magazine

Author	Volume and issue
Title of article	Month and year
Title of magazine	Page numbers

Cantrell, Arthur, "Automatic Teller Is Newest Store Employee," <u>Chain Store Age</u>, XL, No. 2 (September, 1980), 42-57.

Sample data cards might look like this:

Direct quotation

Subject
Quoted material
Source

Electronic banking: <u>problems</u>

"The lack of backup can discourage customer use of electronic banking because there is considerable frustration and inconvenience if there are long interruptions in service. Customers get out of the habit or go elsewhere."
Bill Day, Store Mgr., Sally's Soopers, March 15, 1980.

Paraphrase

Subject
Paraphrased material
Source

Electronic banking: <u>clerk</u> <u>assisted</u> operations

68% cardholders surveyed said they used system and liked being able to cash checks, withdraw or deposit money and transfer funds from one account to another. Many reported having a clerk to help them encouraged more use.

Annual Report, Sally's Soopers, January, 1980. (p. 88)

Note cards work better than notebooks or loose pieces of paper because they are easier to find and handle and can be continually rearranged as needed.

2. For material that doesn't fit on a card (such as photo copies of article or book pages) use file folders, one for each subject heading.

In the beginning of your information gathering, your groups of data for note cards and file folders will probably fall under broad categories. The more you find out about your subject, however, the more sub-topics you will be able to identify; and in thinking about what kind of order these subject blocks should follow, you have already started the process of organizing and outlining.

Getting Input from Employees

Gathering information from employees, whether suggestions, gripes, attitudes or opinions, provides indispensable input for management decision-making. Good, two-way internal communication gets the work done. What's more, effective internal communication both assesses and influences employee morale.

According to Keith Davis:

> Each manager serves as a linking pin connecting his unit with other units to make a chain which will maintain good communication even in large organizations. As with chain links, if one understanding unit has poor communication, those units which depend on it for communication are also weakened.[1]

Most managers recognize upward communication as just as important as downward but they have difficulty recognizing and overcoming the barriers to effective—and *honest*—messages coming up through the hierarchy. "How do our employees *really feel* about the new company health and accident plan?" seems a simple enough question, but the answer is amazingly elusive.

Opinion polls and attitude surveys are commonly used, particularly in large organizations, but they cannot help but be influenced by organizational climate, patterns of employee participation, and accustomed levels of trust and openness. Many a manager has had to scrap a batch of questionnaires after finding out, the hard way, that some of the questions were poorly constructed and therefore elicited ambiguous answers, or the answers to open-ended questions could not be quantified, or that the 30 percent response rate did not provide a true cross section of opinion.

Even when pleased to be asked, employees might not give completely honest answers. If the organizational leadership is autocratic or lacks clear direction, employees might suspect the survey is a gimmick and management has a hidden agenda. Insecure employees might feel that honest answers would put their employment on the line. Even highly competent, totally secure workers have been known to give biased answers in an effort to provide the boss with the answers he or she expects or wants. Out of loyalty, people will answer in ways that make the boss look good, even if they have to stretch the truth.

What can management do to get accurate and useful upward communication? First, the process should be part of the regular communication flow and not a sudden, special project. View an opinion poll as only one of a continuous series of communicative acts. Managers who have nurtured a supportive, cooperative organizational climate that operates *every day* will find their upward communication increasing in volume and improving in quality. "Do I really want to know what is going on and how employees feel? Do I really want to hear the bad news as well as the good?" are questions that managers must continually ask themselves.

Some companies feel they get the most effective upward communication by using oral means—interviews, conferences, and meetings. Depending upon the overall climate once again, as well as the skill of the people involved, face-to-face methods can be highly useful or very threatening to the employee. Some firms use their grievance systems, personnel counselors, and ombudsmen as sources for employee input. Other organizations funnel questions and answers through the company newspaper or newsletter.

No matter which method you choose, employees need to be protected and to be assured that the information volunteered will not be used against them. Moreover, employees need to know that the information supplied is important to management, that it will make a difference, and will be used in decision making. Few employees are fooled by propaganda circulated in the guise of questionnaires or surveys, and willing participation in opinion polls will decrease if it becomes obvious that management has no intention of correcting the problems uncovered.

Getting employee input in written form has both positive and negative aspects. Anonymity is easier to achieve when slips are placed in a Suggestion Box or checks are made on a questionnaire. But some employees hesitate to write something for fear of exposing their lack of facility with spelling or grammar or having their handwriting recognized.

Although instructing people not to sign their names to opinion polls usually encourages honest replies, it doesn't always work that way. For example, in one organization for which I was conducting a training program for middle managers, I asked for some attitudes and opinions on a form sent to participants before the program. My goal was to learn what communication problems the managers were experiencing so that I could tailor the program to meet their specific needs. Because the company required such forms be routed via the participants' supervisors and because it occurred to me that some supervisors might *be* the problem, I requested that no names be supplied on the form. Not many people responded to my questionnaire and when I later asked why, one manager, who seemed to speak for more than himself, said, "Well, since you didn't want my name on the form I decided it wasn't very important, or worth doing!"

In most instances, however, the use of an outside consultant or consulting firm offers one good way of protecting employee identity. Forms can be distributed and collected without being seen by other members of the organization and only compiled responses are made public.

To help you conduct successful attitude surveys or opinion

polls, which is a complex, highly scientific process, here are some suggestions.

Step One. *Define and clarify objectives*. Everyone involved should understand and agree to the purpose of the poll. What is the poll measuring? Generally, polls are used to gather information that does not readily flow upward through channels, such as suggestions for improvement and employee reaction to policy change.

Step Two. *Target the audience*. Will the poll be administered throughout the store or the chain or will the people surveyed be a narrow, select group? Depending on the size of the organization, it may be necessary to query only a sample population, provided the sample is truly representative of the larger group.

Step Three. *Do some pretesting*. Pilot polls conducted among small samples of the ultimate population will save time and money in the long run because they may uncover weaknesses in the proposed questions, the form, the procedures, or the compilation methods. A pretest will point up slanted questions ("You really do like your job here, don't you?") and such problems as questions which lack safeguards against faked answers, or a too-long questionnaire which requires too much lost time.

Step Four. *Finalize the form and format*. An opinion poll usually starts with questions about the employee, such as age, sex, and length of service. The next block of questions, aimed at getting the desired information, may take one or more of the following forms: Agree/Disagree questions, multiple choice questions, items to rank, check lists, and open-ended questions. Here are some examples.

Agree/Disagree: (Check the appropriate place on the continuum.)
The new training program for checkers is well planned.

Strongly Agree	Agree More Than Disagree	Don't Know	Disagree More Than Agree	Strongly Disagree

Multiple Choice: (Check the answer that comes closest to your opinion.)

What do you think of the new district newsletter?

Excellent   Good   Fair   Bad   Terrible

_____

Ranking: (Rank the following aspects of your job, from 1 to 5, in the order of their importance to you.)

_____ Good pay
_____ Opportunities for advancement
_____ Fringe benefits
_____ Constructive criticism
_____ Personal counseling

Check list: (Check all of the factors that apply.)

What were your reasons for deciding to work for our company?
_____ Salary
_____ Our reputation
_____ Location
_____ Working conditions
_____ Opportunities for training
_____ Other

Open-ended:

If you had the opportunity to change any of our company's policies, what is the first change you would make?

_____

Step Five: *Decide how best to administer the survey.* Depending on the size of the organization and its geographical spread, choose between (1) a mail survey to be sent to the office or home; or (2) assembling employees in one location to answer the questions. Whether to use in-house personnel or an outside agency also needs to be decided.

Step Six: *Analyze and publish results.* You or someone on your staff needs to know how to handle statistical formulas, analyses, and procedures that can turn raw data into meaningful information. Has the instrument been tested for validity to make sure it measures what it is supposed to? Decisions also must be made on the best means of broadcasting or distributing the results. Should they be presented in narrative, statistical or graphic form, or a combination?

Step Seven: *Plan for administrative follow-up.* Who will review the data and decide what they mean and what needs to be done? Is corrective action necessary? Should policies be changed? Following such management decisions, all affected personnel should be informed.

If these seven steps seem too long or time-consuming, consider an impartial outside individual or agency. Larger organizations, particularly, will find a professional job more objective as well as more time- and cost-effective.

Summary

Business writing requires clear and relevant information. Sometimes the data we need are already available in our minds or file cabinets. However, if we don't have the necessary information handy, we need to understand *what* facts, opinions, inferences, and judgments to gather, *where* to find them, and *how* best to go about it. Getting honest input from employees represents both a vital and difficult management task.

Note

[1]Keith Davis, *Human Behavior at Work*, 4th ed. (New York: McGraw-Hill Book Company, 1972), p. 385.

6

ORGANIZATION AND STRUCTURE

What goes where?

You may be tempted to skip this chapter because the ideas of planning a format and worse yet, *outlining*, make you uncomfortable. Ever since your elementary school English teacher made you break open sentences and paragraphs into parts and sub-parts, you've resisted the whole process of organization. But "hang in there." You are about to get some tools that will make organizing easier to understand and accomplish.

Why Organization Is Necessary

Without an organization plan, writers proceed from idea to idea something like a dog sniffing from tree to tree. There may be a plan in the dog's itinerary but only he knows what it is. True, some people organize and plan in their heads before they start to write and that's workable for short letters or memos. But more is required for long letters and reports.

One of the reasons that organizing appears to be painful is that it can't be separated from the thinking process. Each time we put ideas into a sequence, we have to understand their relationship; each time we edit and rewrite, we make decisions about why one word is better than another. We also try to predict what the reader will understand from the end product. Putting similar materials together and outlining represent exercises in logic. We have to think through every stage.

In an article titled "Clear writing means clear thinking means . . ." Marvin H. Swift describes the step-by-step process a manager went through in writing a memorandum to his staff about not using the office copy machine for personal purposes. The first version was accusatory and blunt, but helped the manager blow off steam. Fortunately, he didn't send it. As he went through several revisions, he found that his main problem was not in the writing but in thinking through the policy he was writing about. In the end, not only the memo but the policy was considerably altered.[1]

Not only does the development of clear organization help the writer, it gives invaluable help to the reader. If the reader can see a pattern, he or she will read more efficiently and also concentrate better. An organizational pattern provides a road map to help the reader quickly see the significance of the starting point, the destination, and the route in between.

In directionless writing, the ideas come out like a collection of beads, all apparently the same size. But an organization pattern provides the string to make connections between beads and to identify key beads from less important ones.

Goals of Organization

Writers actually start the organization process when they decide on their purpose and then start to make choices about material, development, style, and language to help achieve the purpose. Although the material at this point may have both an unwieldy and fuzzy shape, nevertheless a form begins to emerge.

The first and most important goal of organization is to turn a hodgepodge of material into a unified structure. Such structures needn't be highly complex. In fact, the more effective organization patterns are simple enough to be instantly recognized and understood by the reader.

A second goal is to find the focus, the right perspective to spotlight the significance of the subject as a whole. What slant or theme will provide the peg upon which the whole framework will hang? Sometimes what originally seemed like an insignificant feature becomes the needed underlying common denominator that makes everything fall into place. Moreover, what seems like a flaw can sometimes be turned into a unifying asset. For example, I once interviewed a famous opera singer for a newspaper. After the excitement of the encounter, when I tried to write my story, I was struck by the dullness of the conversation that appeared in my notes. I realized that in my inexperience as an interviewer, I had asked mostly uninspired, overworked questions and had consequently received vapid, prosaic answers. I was about to throw the notes away when it struck me that my theme could be the very triteness of the interview as something often faced by famous people. It worked.

Another goal is to find the thesis or the main point. Sometimes, but not always, identical to the theme or slant previously discussed, the main point may emerge as a separate idea deserving of emphasis. Newspaper headlines, that attempt to distill the story's main point in cryptic phrases give the reader thesis statements. Look for a thesis in connection with your purpose.

Let's try an example to illustrate the distinction between focus, purpose, and thesis. Suppose you are asked to prepare a report on the use of generic foods in your chain. When you begin to organize the material gathered, you might write at the top of the page:

SUBJECT: Use of generic foods in our chain
PURPOSE: To inform top management that sales have been high and store managers report favorable customer response.

THESIS: It was a good move for our chain to institute a special section of generic foods.

FOCUS: We began the program because our major competitor advertised "No Name Brands." Since we needed a different approach, we emphasize "Little Known Brands."

A final goal of organization is to achieve the following characteristics of style:

Balance: segments harmoniously arranged and in appropriate proportions

Coherence: logical consistency between and among ideas and blocks of material

Contrast: changes of pace and visual effects to avoid monotony (such as from formal to informal, from restful to dynamic)

Emphasis: important points receive appropriate stress; minor ideas are subordinated; irrelevant details are eliminated

Unity: parts add up to a single, major effect

The Process of Organizing

Once you have finished gathering the information you need and your desk looks littered with books, magazines, note cards, notebooks, and files, what are you going to do with all that stuff? All you need to do now is assimilate, interpret, analyze, and synthesize, and as if that weren't enough, you then need to distill everything into a unified, coherent, highly readable piece of writing. This point in the process, where the task seems insurmountable, has given organizing a bad name.

Many writing textbooks will have the student leap from gathering material to outlining it. But not so fast! There are some important activities that writers should do in between gathering and outlining.

1. Do some preliminary sorting and reviewing of the material you have. Skim through it all again; refresh your memory on what you have gathered. Do your preliminary classifications still hold up or now that you know more about the subject, do other categories seem more useful? Shuffle the cards into a different order. Perhaps you have them alphabetically arranged by problem area. Try rearranging them into a chronological or some other order.

2. At the same time that you mechanically sort material, you also mentally sort and rearrange. Back off and think about the subject as a whole. Rearrange the focus and ideas in your head. This process, which involves mostly sitting and thinking, should not be skipped on the grounds that you don't have time. Allowing ideas to roll around and percolate improves both writing and organizing.

Activities 1 and 2 may produce the perspective or slant you need to begin the process of picking an organization pattern. But if not, a third step has proven successful.

3. Brainstorm about the subject. Put down on paper, in abbreviated form, and in no particular order, all the ideas you can think of that relate to your subject and purpose. Resist evaluating as you go; don't think of ideas as "good" or "bad," "relevant" or "irrelevant" at this point. Just put them all down. Once you have your list complete, *then* evaluate.

Look at the list as a whole. Do any patterns suggest themselves? Would the material fit into a problem-solution pattern? Does the information exist over a period of time so that a chronological or historical framework would be appropriate? Do you see things on the list that you already know should be discarded? Are you tempted to hang on to a less important point because it's a favorite of yours or just because you have more material about it than about the others? What relationships do you see between the aspects listed?

With the help of the mechanical and mental sorting and brainstorming, most material will almost seem to be organizing itself. When the process goes well, a feeling of rightness, of inevitability comes through.

Although we have been discussing organization patterns, you still aren't ready to outline. Final selection of the pattern cannot be made until you have made some more decisions.

4. Identify the thesis, or the main idea. Have you found the heart of the matter about which you want to write?

5. Identify the people who will read what you write. What information do they most need and want?

6. Decide on a specific purpose. What effect do you hope to have on the reader? Are you trying to inform, to actuate, to persuade—or a combination?

7. Now select the organizational pattern that best fits the material, focus, thesis, reader, and purpose.

What is an organizational pattern? It is a unifying theme or way of thinking that runs throughout the material.

Following are ten potential patterns that may be used either as the overall framework or to organize sub-parts. For example, you may decide that your report best fits into a Problem-Solution Pattern (Number 8) and that the events in the subsections should be handled in the order they occurred (Number 1). Although combinations are fine, be careful not to hop and skip from pattern to pattern because that gives the effect of no pattern. Choose one consistent pattern for overall; and if you use other patterns for subsections, stay with the same one throughout the section.

Patterns of Organization

Type	*Sample Outline*
1. *Time or Chronological* Events or details are arranged with respect to time: from the past to the present; from the present to the past; or from the present to the future.	I Main idea II Events or aspects in a chrono-logical order III Conclusion

Type	*Sample Outline*
2. *Space* Material is arranged according to space: east to west; far to near; top to bottom; or inside to outside.	I Thing or concept II Overview of topography III Details according to a space arrangement IV Summary or conclusion
3. *Enumeration or Classification* Separate details are listed to support or explain an assertion or generalization. Often used for a unit within another pattern.	I Main idea II Numbered or classified details III Summary or conclusion
4. *Who-What-When-Where-How-Why* Follows the journalistic style of quickly answering the six most important questions.	I Main idea II Who, what, when, where, how, why III Conclusion
5. *Specific Instance* Illustrates a key idea by telling an anecdote or describing an incident or event.	I Main idea II Detailed anecdote or illustration III Conclusion
6. *Comparison and/or Contrast* Two or more elements are compared for similarity and/or contrasted for differences	I Items compared/contrasted II Summary of similarities and/or differences III Conclusion

Type		*Sample Outline*
7. *Cause and Effect* A point of view or opinion is supported by reasoning, with the material arranged according to causes and results.	I	Causes of an event, factor, or circumstance
	II	Results from these causes
	III	Conclusion
8. *Problem-Solution* The problem is diagnosed and the best way to solve it selected from potential solutions.	I	Analysis of problem
	II	Possible solutions
	III	Elimination of all but best solution
	IV	Best solution
	V	Conclusion
9. *Motivated Sequence*[2] Used when the purpose is to persuade	I	Get attention
	II	Establish need or problem
	III	Show how to satisfy need or solve problem
	IV	Help readers visualize results
	V	Call for action
	VI	Summary or conclusion
10. *All-Purpose* Effective unless overworked.	I	Get attention
	II	Overview of subject
	III	Fill in specific information
	IV	Summary and conclusion

From this quick overview of ten potential patterns, let's now examine some ways the same general subject matter could be arranged according to different patterns. Suppose you need to do a report about retail managers' salaries. Perhaps your material would best fit into a *chronological* pattern, which looks at salary changes over time.

66

Job level	Average Manager's Salary		
	1960	1970	1980
Store Manager	$___	$___	$___
Assistant Manager	$___	$___	$___
Unit Manager	$___	$___	$___

Or you may organize your data into a *space* pattern, showing comparative salary figures for different parts of the country:

Job level	Average Manager's Salary Regions of the U.S.			
	East	West	North	South
Store Manager	$___	$___	$___	$___
Assistant Manager	$___	$___	$___	$___
Unit Manager	$___	$___	$___	$___

Maybe you will prefer a *cause-effect* pattern, showing what factors seem principally responsible for major changes from time to time:

Average Manager's Salary

1. Factors that have affected salary:

    A. Economic health, inflation, cost of living
    B. Managers generally have more education, training, and experience today
    C. Retail stores and chains are now more professionally managed and are growing in size and influence
    D. Salary scales are now more scientifically and equitably determined.

Or you may use a *comparison* pattern, showing how managers' salaries relate to those of comparably trained people in other professions:

Average Manager's Salary
Compared to Other Professions

	Accountant	Plumber	Police Officer	Teacher	Manager
1960	$____	$____	$____	$____	$____
1970	$____	$____	$____	$____	$____
1980	$____	$____	$____	$____	$____

Outlining Revisited

Surprise! This section will not deal with the rights and wrongs of outlining. Instead, it identifies the outline as a tool that comes in many shapes. Some people are intimidated because they aren't sure whether Roman numerals come first or letters. Who cares? The purpose of the outline is to give *you* a blueprint for *your use* so you can devise any system that works for you.

Think of the outline as the backbone of your material. Think of it, always, as tentative. Avoid the trap of feeling stuck with whatever pattern you first select. Redoing or rearranging an outline is a lot easier than rewriting a whole manuscript.

With the aid of an outline, even a sketchy one, you begin to see how your ideas can be segregated, coordinated, and subordinated to achieve balance and proportion. For a stab at outlining, you might try this format which works for many of the organization patterns. But don't worry about the symbols or making it exact.

Topic or subject:
Thesis or main idea:
Purpose:
I. First main topic
    A. First subtopic
      1. First supporting point or example
      2. Second supporting point or example
    B. Second subtopic
      1. First supporting point or example
      2. Second supporting point or example

68

II. Second main topic
  A. First subtopic
    1. First supporting point or example
    2. Second supporting point or example
    3. Third supporting point or example
III. Third main topic
  A. First subtopic
  B. Second subtopic
    1. First supporting point or example
    2. Second supporting point or example
  C. Third subtopic

In the above example, each item has its place and its relationship to the other aspects, You can tell at a glance which points are most important, which have more value than others. Notice, however, that not all subtopics have supporting points (as in III-A) and it's okay to have just one subtopic without having to balance it with another one (as in II-A).

Whether to use Roman numerals or letters is not important. What *is* important is giving ideas at the same level relatively similar weight. For example, in the sample outline, all the Roman numerals should be the most important topics and parallel to each other. All the A's and B's under a main topic should be of fairly equal weight.

Sometimes your Roman numeral I will include your introductory material. Other times, it works better to have your introductory and concluding material *outside* the outline. Most writers like to work on those last, anyway, after they see what basic shape the material takes.

With an outline as your guide, you are free to write quickly and develop your thoughts one at a time without fear of leaving some out or in repeating yourself. If a tangential idea occurs during the writing, it can be checked against the outline and either inserted or abandoned. Writing can proceed with fewer mental distractions.

In the finished manuscript, the outlined points will, of course, not always be labeled or numbered. But where headings are useful to the reader, they will follow the same relative weight and proportion that the outline did.

Type size and spacing can be used to clarify the relative importance of headings, as well as the material that follows. In the following chart, which includes directions that might be given to a typist or typesetter, "caps" means capital letters, "lower case" means uncapped letters, and "letter space" means put a space between letters.

STYLE FOR HEADS AND SUBHEADS
(TO INDICATE RELATIVE IMPORTANCE)

1.	M A J O R H E A D I N G S	centered, caps, letter-space; triple space above and below
2.	IMPORTANT HEADINGS	centered; caps, triple space above and below
3. MAIN HEADINGS		flush with left margin, caps, double space above and below
4. Sub- or Lesser Headings		flush with left margin, caps and lower case, underscored with solid line

5. Least important headings. These are flush with the left margin, first word only capped, only words underscored. Copy proceeds from heading without special spacing.

Supporting Ideas and Details

Now you need to put flesh and muscle (but not fat) on your skeleton outline. Your main points and major subtopics are probably quite general and to keep them from becoming sweeping generalizations, you must support them, illuminate them, and pin them down with specifics. Supporting material comes in many forms. You may use actions, ideas, emotional attitudes, impressions, or statistical data.

Here are the six most common forms of supporting material.

1. Explanation, description, illustration

Amazingly few ideas can stand alone as completely self-explanatory. Abstract terms, in particular, need expanding, defining, clearcut examples and descriptions in order for the reader to know what *you* mean by them. As an example, ask the next five people you meet to define something like "free enterprise" or "democracy." You discover that *words* don't mean, *people* mean.

One useful form of explanation shows relationships among and between ideas. Another uses the kind of narrative in which you tell a story, use an illustrative fable, describe historical incidents, or tell a humorous or moving anecdote.

Sometimes one illustration details a dramatized scene; sometimes it tells a story about a connected series of events; sometimes it describes a brief specific instance. In whatever form used, illustrations help make the material vivid and recognizable to the reader; they can be the most powerful kind of supporting information.

> This management problem is reminiscent of Columbus' experience, starting out without knowing where he was going, arriving at an unknown place, and returning without knowing where he had been!

Writing like this is far more effective than using arguments, statistics, or multiple facts because it brings the point into sharp focus, and does it with a grin.

71

2. Analogy or comparison

When you use material of this sort you point out similarities between what is known or believed and what is not; you use the known to make the unknown more understandable or believable. This method helps the reader see how an idea, person, event, or thing is like another.

> The store is laid out in a half-circle with the aisles moving outward from the service desk as the spokes of a wheel move out from the hub.

Other analogies can be drawn by using *contrasts* instead of or along with comparisons. Ideas, people, events, or things are contrasted for their differences. Here also you identify the unknown by means of the known, but by telling what the unknown is *not*.

> The new store will be laid out in a half-circle in contrast to the older square or rectangular buildings. Instead of plain concrete walls, the new store will have a combination of steel, glass, and brick.

3. Quotations or testimony

Often your ideas will carry more weight and exert more influence if they are supported by quotations from others, particularly those who are experts in the subject. The notion of "expert," however, needs some cautionary advice. Some people make the mistake of equating prominence with wisdom. Although members of Congress have access to more information than the average person, they do not automatically qualify as experts in every field. Famous people are often quoted but their fame or wealth do not make them experts.

Questions you should ask yourself before quoting a so-called expert are: (a) Does this person have special experience or training in this field? (b) Does this person have first-hand knowledge? (c) Does this person have a vested interest in this field that would cause him or her to be more biased than other people?

Testimony you use as supporting material may be *directly quoted* (The store manager said, "Generic foods have brought in a lot of new business to our store.") or *paraphrased* (The store manager said the addition of generic foods to the store had increased sales.). Testimony may be factual, opinions, attitudes, or from literary or journalistic sources.

4. Restatement and/or repetition

When you want to add force to an idea, try restating it in a different form. "In other words, . . ." introduces the same thought but in different form or language. Occasionally, the same thought in the same words, or repetition, can also be used for added emphasis. Both restatement and repetition allow the reader time to absorb the full meaning. What's more, they are useful devices with which to snag the reader who skims. If the reader overlooked the point the first time, he or she might notice it when it shows up again in restated or repeated form.

5. Factual information

Facts, figures, and statistics frequently help writers back up their assertions. An assertion may sound like fact ("The quality of new hirees at our store this year has been poor.") but needs evidence or proof before the reader will accept it as probable or likely. There is a whale of a difference between "getting facts down on paper" and *communicating* information to the reader.

Fact was defined in Chapter 5, in the discussion about facts, inferences, opinions, and judgments. *Figures* are numbers used to explain and clarify ("Three new stores were opened last year.") whereas *statistics* are groups of facts or figures that have been

73

assembled, classified, and tabulated in order to present or substantiate findings or assertions.

Statistics enable you to present and compare data on complex matters but writers should beware of two critical problems connected with their use.

First, *whose* statistics are they? The opportunity for distortion is exemplified by that old (but pertinent) adage: Figures can't lie but liars can figure. The nineteenth-century British statesman, Benjamin Disraeli, said, "There are three kinds of lies: lies, damned lies and statistics."

Second, figures and statistics, particularly in large doses, make hard going for the reader, who may make a habit of skipping over columns of figures and looking, instead, for explanations in the text that tell what the figures *mean*. Most readers handle words and pictures far better than numbers or columns of figures.

For now, let's summarize by saying that facts should be used copiously, but figures and statistics sparingly. If numerical data are important to your writing, then be sure to clarify what they are based on, where they came from and, above all, what they mean.

6. Visual aids

Charts, maps, graphs, and diagrams can greatly assist in clarifying your statistical material and in making other points as well. A discussion of cost percentages, for example, can be quickly visualized by the reader if you show him or her a *pie chart* where the percentages are represented by different sizes of pie slices. Changes in dollar income over the years can be made more meaningful by showing them on a *bar graph* or *pictograph*. (A pictograph is a picture that uses simple drawings to compare two or more sets of numbers.) See Figures 1 and 2.

Interestingly, though, readers don't automatically know how to understand charts and graphs, or even drawings or photographs. They often miss the point of the visual. Although a picture may be worth a thousand words, it often takes more than a

74

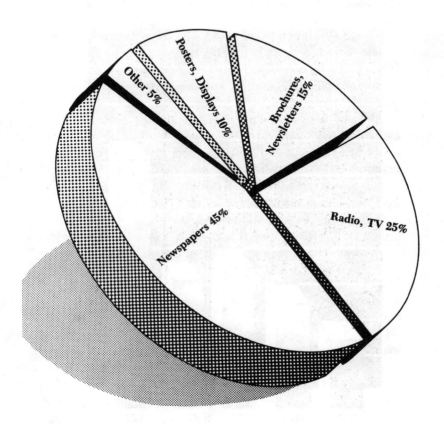

Estimated Distribution of Advertising Allocation

1980 Advertising Budget Sally Sooper's Chain

Figure 1. Pie Chart

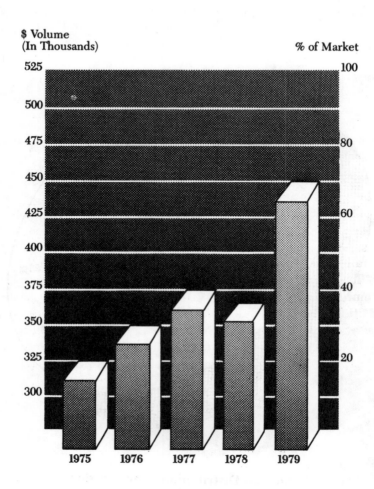

Annual Gross Sales (All Stores)
Sally Sooper's Chain

Figure 2. Bar Graph

thousand words to explain what the picture means to the writer and why he or she included it in the report. For visual material to effectively support your expository writing, you need to tell the reader how to look at the visual and why. In other words, to be safe, tell the reader what to see and what it means.

Visuals work best if they aren't too complicated, if they tell the story quickly, and help the reader *see* your point. Don't overwork charts and graphs; use them only if your narrative discussion needs them to be made more clear and compelling.

Transitions and Connectives

The last part of organizing is to provide signposts to help the reader see where your writing is headed and from which direction it has come. One advantage of a good outline is that transitions naturally emerge from the order in which the points occur.

To tell if you need more or better transitions, check the beginning of your paragraphs and sentences. Do they sound repetitious? Is there a dull sameness about the way sentences and paragraphs are organized? Since the evaluation and addition of transitions usually occur as part of the editing and rewriting process, you will find more on this subject, plus a detailed list of useful connective words and phrases, in Chapter 8.

Summary

Organization exists as both an integral and vital part of writing and may seem painful because it cannot be separated from the thinking process. Through organization, both the writer and the reader can detect a structure, focus, and the thesis or main idea. The process of organizing begins with both a mechanical and mental sorting before an organizational pattern (or patterns) can be selected. Once the pattern has been translated into a preliminary outline, one or more of six kinds of supporting material can be added and finally, transitions or connectives can be used to link up sections and ideas effectively.

Notes

[1]Marvin H. Swift, "Clear writing means clear thinking means . . . ," *Harvard Business Review*, 51 (1973), 59-62.

[2]Adapted from Alan H. Monroe and Douglas Ehninger, *Principles and Types of Speech Communication*, 8th ed. (Glenview: Scott, Foresman and Company, 1978).

7

LANGUAGE AND MEANING

Can I help it if what you said isn't what you meant?

Perhaps the most interesting aspect of language—any language in current use—is the way it lives as a constantly changing process. Those of us brought up on strict grammatical rules and "proper" usage can't help wincing when nouns and verbs do not agree or when traditional meanings get turned around. Yet *usage* is what changes a language, not its rules.

For example, common usage rather than logic made "helped prepare" acceptable but "assisted prepare" unacceptable. English teachers for years have been trying to get us to use "whom." Despite their efforts, the use of whom has so dwindled that "To whom am I speaking?" sounds pompous and artificial, while "Who am I speaking to?" sounds fine and familiar. By the way each of us uses (or doesn't use) words and by the way we follow (or don't follow) grammatical rules, we help shape the language and cast votes on whether or not new terms and forms will eventually become commonly accepted.

A current struggle to update our language involves equalizing sexist terms. While the notion that both men and women should not be called by strictly masculine labels (postman, policeman, fireman) is valid, some people go to comical lengths to try to correct the problem. Take the word "host," which is already nicely sexless, being neither masculine or feminine. For writers who find "host" not precise enough, we already have the fine word, "hostess," defined as a female host. Yet the new word "hostperson" has actually begun to appear! Who needs it? Similarly, the word "foreman" can be balanced by "forewoman," and the only time we need "foreperson" is when the sex of a person is unknown.

If a group of men and women decides to elect a leader, that as yet unknown individual can accurately be called a "chairperson." But after the election, why not refer to the winner as either a chair*man* or a chair*woman?* Although the list of absurd "personhoods" gets longer daily, my favorite, to date, is "Ride 'em, cowperson!"

Language uses symbols that represent something else; the word is not the thing it represents. The word "food store," doesn't look like a food store, sound like a food store, or smell like a food store, but it means food store because we recognize it as the symbol for a food store. Words, as symbols on paper, can take on a somewhat arbitrary, objective symbolic shape; the *meanings* of those words, however, can only be subjective and personal to the reader. Messages come from the outside; meaning comes from the inside. Your readers will derive meaning from what you write, but only based upon *their* experience, attitudes, values, and needs, not yours. As noted before, words don't mean, people mean.

Accepting the fact that no two people can ever perceive a meaning in exactly the same way prevents us from always placing the blame for misunderstanding on the other person. What's more, understanding the private and personal nature of meaning helps us develop patience as we keep trying to find better ways to clarify meanings. We learn to build on common experiences as bases for agreement and understanding, and through trial and error, also recognize words and phrases better left unwritten.

Nothing so clearly reflects your personality as the way you select and use language. You already have your own unique style that needs only to be developed and improved.

This chapter will not consist of tut-tutting about the horrors of the split infinitive or the mangled metaphor but will focus on *communication*. Spotlights will shine on some of the enemies of effective communication, such as awkward or disjointed writing; and there *will* be a brief look at the most common grammatical mistakes, not because of rules but because mistakes interfere with communication. Since readers equate sloppy writing with sloppy thinking, you cannot go too far beyond the bounds of what they, the readers, consider acceptable usage.

Language-Centered Problems

1. Vague, ambiguous writing

The story goes that Napoleon's three rules for transmitting messages were "Be clear! Be clear! Be clear!" Most of us feel certain that we *are* being clear, forgetting that the more we know about a subject, the harder it is to identify with the needs of a reader who knows little or nothing. Concepts and facts that we live with and consider important become abundantly obvious *to us*. How come stupid readers can't follow our intended meaning?

Unclear language comes out either as *vague, ambiguous,* or *equivocal*.

Vague words lack parameters, leaving definitions wide open to interpretation. Examples are "middle age" and "senior citizen," which each of us can define to suit ourselves (and our own age brackets).

Ambiguous words are those with more than one meaning. Examples are "fast" (as in speed, color, or tied?), "round" (as in shape, beef, or trip?), and "top" (toy, lid, or summit?). Simple words such as these can usually be clarified by how they are used in context. This is not true of less simple, more abstract language.

Equivocal terms are those that are deliberately vague, where the writer doesn't want the exact meaning detected. We can all think of examples from the realms of politics, government, and international diplomacy.

During a recent press conference, a federal energy official said, "Our oil shortage is only moderate in the near term." When a puzzled reporter asked him if near term meant a few weeks, the official said in an annoyed tone, "No, it means six to eight months." While the official may not have been deliberately equivocal, he certainly gets a prize for vagueness.

Another source of unclear writing comes from *abstract* terms. True, much of our language depends on words that group concepts, things, or people under categories. This saves time. Abstractions make it unnecessary to separate and label each item in the category. When writing about "managers," for instance, we can assume that most readers understand that not all managers are the same and that we refer to their comparable functions or responsibilities.

But the word "managers" is too broad for complete clarity. Our communication becomes more clear when we bring the term down the abstraction ladder[1] and make it "store managers." By this we signal the reader that we mean to leave out other kinds of managers, such as those in charge of restaurants or corporations. There is still room for misunderstanding, though, unless we pin down the reference to "retail food store managers." Understanding increases as we become more and more specific. "Retail food store managers in the Sally's Soopers Chain" narrows the reference even more. At the bottom of the abstraction ladder would be the most specific reference possible, "Rob Jenkins, manager of the Elmville store of the Sally's Soopers Chain."

Obviously, the higher the level of abstraction, the more opportunity for misunderstanding. Words like *conveyance* (airplane or wheelbarrow?) and *livestock* (cows, pigs, chickens?) are highly abstract. Although the writer of these words might have a specific image in mind, the broad terms give the writer little or no control over the reader's images. Far better for the writer to refer to a Cadillac purring up to the door or a horse named Rex than to leave the reader swimming in a sea of uncertainties.

That innocuous little neuter pronoun, "it," becomes another villain that can cause vague, ambiguous writing. Although "it" is a highly useful word, "it" creates problems if the reader can't tell what object or event is referred to. "It is necessary to go to the district office" leaves the reader wondering "Necessary to whom? Why?" "It was reported that . . ." makes the reader puzzle over who the mysterious, unnamed reporter was. "Managing a meat department or stocking a bakery unit is hard work. I wish I was learning how to do it better." "It" in this case can refer to either meat managing, bakery stocking, or managing in general.

Not only does the indefinite "it" cause unclear messages, starting sentences with "It is . . ." leads to the additional problem of *passive* language. Active verbs spark interest and command attention. Compare "It is my belief that . . ." with the punchier, "I believe."

Here are some additional examples:

Active (the subject of the sentence acts)	**Passive** (the subject of the sentence is acted upon)
The manager scolded the clerk.	The clerk was scolded by the manager.
I did not drop the carton.	The carton was not dropped by me.
We did not expect to win the case.	It was not expected by us that we would win the case.

Don't get the impression, however, that you should never use the passive voice. Sometimes passive verbs work best for emphasis, particularly when the receiver of the action is more important than the subject who acts. As an example, "The manager was threatened by a recently fired stock clerk," achieves more effective emphasis than "A recently fired stock clerk threatened the manager." Trying too hard to avoid the passive may create clumsy constructions and detract from your intended emphasis and meaning. In general, however, active verbs have a way of grabbing the reader, while passive verbs just seem to lie there.

Slang and *jargon* also contribute to vague, ambiguous writing. Slang or colloquial phrases can be amusing and colorful; people invent and repeat new slang in order to sound vivid, original, and "with it." What's more, many slang terms eventually end up as very respectable words. Consider how much "cloning," "macho," and "biodegradable" have recently added to the language.

But slang rarely fits in business writing for two reasons: (1) Popular slang terms have a tendency to sound flippant and, therefore, unbusinesslike. Readers of business letters and reports may get a negative impression about the writer or the firm if informal slang is used. Moreover, when correctly used, slang should be put in quotation marks to show that the writer knows the words are not currently considered good usage, and this only highlights them further. (2) Slang is usually taken up as a fad and then quickly dropped when newer terms come along. Spoken slang gives zest and currency to what you say but written slang remains behind after the fad has passed. Remember all those words and phrases from the Watergate scandals, like "stonewalling," "expletive deleted," "no longer operative," and "at this point in time"? Reports with those catch phrases now sound very dated.

Jargon results from technical or vocational vocabularies which become over-specialized. Almost every profession has its own jargon, which has the virtue of providing communication shortcuts. People save time by using jargon instead of endlessly describing or explaining. Insiders can successfully communicate with jargon; outsiders are usually left in the dark. (Paranoid outsiders suspect that deliberately leaving them in the dark is the main reason for jargon.)

Doctors have their own jargon but cannot understand engineers' shop talk. Pipefitters and school teachers and grocery store personnel all have their own peculiar and specialized jargon. When we become accustomed to an inside lingo, we no longer recognize it as jargon that needs explaining to others.

For example, while doing my research in a large supermarket, I overheard a sentence that was at first meaningless to me. "Tell the third man to get someone to throw aisle three and face aisle fourteen." Translation (for outsiders like me): "Third man" refers to the ranking person in charge after the manager and assistant manager. "Throw the aisle" means put items on the shelf, and "face the aisle" means bring all items forward on the shelves so the shelves look full.

Government forms and reports can be jungles of jargon, commonly called "gobbledygook." Favorite forms end in "ate," "ize," or "wise." Cerebrate and ideate become substitutes for think (honest!). Projects must be optimized and finalized, report-wise, before being journalized. The reader wonders if the whole matter is useful-wise or even wise-wise.

Let's hope none of us gets caught "fuzzifying" material, which means to deliberately present a matter in terms that permit "adjustive" interpretation. Public figures fuzzify when they don't know what they're talking about or when they want to enunciate a non-position in the guise of a position. For examples, listen to the TV news or pick up a newspaper. Other examples can be found in advertising signs and copy. I remember seeing a large sign in Reno, Nevada, in front of a high rise apartment building under construction. Although the sign said the apartments would be "Luxurious and Intimate," I decided from the looks of the building that the apartments would really be *expensive* and *small*.

If jargon is clear to all its users, it works. Too often, however, even insiders such as new employees and people from other divisions are baffled. Jargon can obscure thought by relying on technical terms and acronyms (words formed out of initials) and also by circling around the idea instead of moving directly to the point with short, commonly understood words. Use jargon sparingly, and only for in-house, in-store matters. Don't use it as the lazy way out of the work necessary for successful, clear writing.

Sometimes not only words but whole sentences lack clarity. Such statements, dropped into the material in a way that leaves the reader going, "Huh?" occur when the writer fails to include the whole thought or answer the question "why?" These are samples taken from real business reports:

Since that time our reports ceased being accurate. (Why?)
We are again getting new name badges. (Why?)

The EEO Master Report has continued to show incorrect labor codes. (Why?)

2. Old-fashioned, overblown writing

When beginning business writers are given an assignment, they often look in the files for a sample to use as a guide. Although not a bad practice since it's the quickest way for new managers to learn about accepted forms and formats, following file copies can also result in copying the language used by predecessors. If not alert to this possibility, the new manager may acquire a supply of overworked and tired stock phrases that no longer communicate.

Chances are those archaic "Yrs. of the 14th inst. received" and "Contents duly noted" expressions will be recognized as belonging in the last century. But stuffy, old-fashioned phrases still persist in today's business writing. Although they are easy to fall back on, they give the reader a feeling that the letter was originally mass-produced and never updated. Such letters have the insensitivity of the bridal consultant who used a stock sign-off in her letter to a new bride: "We hope we may serve you very soon again."

Here is only a short sampling of the many business clichés to be avoided. Add your own most disliked, non-communicative words and phrases to the list.

According to our records
Assuring you of our prompt attention
Beg to advise
Deem it advisable
Enclosed please find
Have before me your letter of
Kindly advise
Per your instructions
Please find enclosed
Pursuant to your request
Thanking you in advance

Trusting to hear from you soon
Under separate cover
We are in receipt of
With your kind permission

Another misuse of language stems from a pompous, over-blown style, in which the writer seems determined to use as many words as possible. Going the long way around, or belaboring the obvious, only adds flab to the material, not understanding. Here are some examples.

Excess wording	*Better*
a large number of	many (or tell how many)
as a matter of fact	actually
at an early date	soon
at that time	then
at the present time	now
because of the fact that	because
be in receipt of	get
by the time that	when
by virtue of the fact that	because
come in contact with	contact, meet
come to a decision as to	decide
continue on	continue
due to the fact that	because
during the time that	while
each and every	each
first and foremost	first
for the purpose of	for
get an understanding of	understand
have the capability of	can
in reference to	about
in spite of the fact that	although
in the event that	if
in the vast majority of cases	generally
in the very near future	soon
in very few instances	seldom

it will be advisable for him to	he should
make an analysis of	analyze
make every effort to	try hard
make use of	use
merged together	merged
more and more frequently	increasingly
of the nature of	like
on the grounds that	since, because
pertaining to	about
prior to	before
proceed ahead	proceed
reach a conclusion as to	decide
refer back to	refer
regardless of the fact that	although
subsequent to	after
take into account	consider
that is to say	that is
we are now in the process of	we are now
whether or not	whether
with respect to	about

Excess words abound in platitudes which, because they have been worked to death, sidetrack meaning. Avoid figures of speech such as "tide of battle," "ship of state," "irony of fate," and "sharp as a tack." Cast out clichés like "true colors," "broad daylight," "just desserts," and "ripe old age."

3. Wrong words and wounded words

Someone once lamented, "What can you expect of a language in which 'fat chance' and 'slim chance' mean the same thing?" Whoever that was had a point. (There's also "flammable" and "inflammable.") But the substitution of a wrong word for a correct word, and the twisting of meaning which makes a correct word wrong in its usage are constant problems to plague both writers and readers.

My theory is that many people who make wrong word choices do so because they can't *hear* the difference between two or more similar-sounding words. Don't you know people who take others "for granite," as well as business writers who refer to the end of the "physical year" when costs will be figured on a "per capital" basis? A congressman recently proposed that an "anec-dote" be passed for the crime of child pornography but he didn't want to be "misconscrewed." Then there's my friend who hangs her curtains on "traveler's rods," likes "French Prudential" furni-ture, frequently gets "sidetrapped," suffers from "high-perten-sion," worries about a "be-nine tumor," and tries to reach the "pinochle of success."

People who misspell "quantity" by making it "quanity," or turn "nuclear" into "nucular" or use "of" instead of "have" (as in the football player's comment, "He might of gotten pushed into me") are writing and spelling the way they pronounce. Language-training specialists report we can speak only what we can hear. Perhaps, then, the best solution is not spelling classes but listen-ing courses.

Amazing verbal idiosyncrasies occur when people blithely make up their own versions of words. A weatherman recently advised motorists to watch for ice where roads hadn't been "main-tenanced." What's wrong with "maintained," since "mainte-nance" is a noun not a verb? An airline spokesman announced that a strike had caused passengers to be "disaccommodated." Really!

"Hopefully" has been incorrectly used so much we are prob-ably stuck with it. Strictly writing, "hopefully" can only mean that the writer is in a hopeful state of mind, not that he or she hopes something will happen. "Hopefully, the report will be finished on time," makes language purists squirm because reports can't hope; only people can hope. Only time and usage will tell about that one.

"Disinterested" does *not* mean "uninterested," it means "without bias on either side." Writers persist in using "I feel" when they mean "I think" or "I believe." You can't "suspicion" something; all you can do is "suspect." And appropriately saved for last on what could be an endless list is "nauseous." You might be "nauseated" but if you *really* mean you are "nauseous," then you are disgusting to others.

4. Silly sentences

Over the years, I have collected silly sentences, which are made silly by lack of logic, double meanings, or a misplaced phrase. Truly, I have not fabricated any of the following examples. They have all been in print or spoken publicly.

Lack of logic or mangled metaphors

Let's not beat a dead horse to death.
Those seeds you planted have come home to roost.
His face is not a household word.
The future isn't what it used to be.
If you don't receive this letter, please let me know.
That's so unbelievable it defies my belief.

Double meanings

I passed this letter through our attorneys.
We have been authorized to make monthly advances to Ms. Schultz.
The panel was made up of a banker, an economics professor, a congressman, and a small businesswoman.

Misplaced phrases

A private passenger vehicle is one registered to an individual with a gross weight of less than 8,000 pounds.
The dress designer explained about doing people around the country's clothes.
The man caught the disease which is spread by mosquitoes, while vacationing in the area.

Upon arrival on the scene, the house was fully involved in the fire.

It was a three-year-old Attorney General's opinion.

5. Pitfalls in grammar, spelling, and punctuation

No one expects business writers to be model grammarians and we all should be forgiven occasional slips. Some lucky writers have secretaries who edit out mistakes, but most of us have to be our own editors. Mistakes in grammar, spelling, and punctuation, unfortunately, communicate qualities about the author which he or she does not intend. What's more, readers who know correct usage may miss the writer's message entirely because of distracting mistakes.

Four most common grammatical mistakes

A. *Agreement between subject and verb*. The subject and its verb must agree in number and in person: a singular subject requires a singular verb; a plural or compound subject requires a plural verb. "He *was* here yesterday; they *were* here the day before."

Recently, I was surprised to see a food store ad in my local paper with a bold headline proclaiming RECENTLY REDUCED PRICES AND THERE'S HUNDREDS MORE. If the ad writer had left out the hundreds, "There's more" would have been okay. But since "there's" means *there is*, the writer should have made it "There *are* hundreds more."

Most of us know the basics about subject and verb agreement but get into trouble when using compound subjects, collective nouns, or a series.

Correct	*Reason*
One case of canned dog food or two cases of dog biscuits *are*	When a compound subject has both a singular (one case) and

91

Correct	*Reason*
needed to fill out the display.	plural (two cases) components, whichever one is closer to the verb governs.
After the committee *convenes,* the members *discuss* the report.	Collective nouns (committee, staff, group) take singular verbs.
A series of problems *was* responsible for lower sales.	The subject is "series," which is singular, not "problems."
Neither Pete nor Henry *was* available.	Singular persons are being contrasted.

Noun and verb agreement problems also crop up when we try to avoid "he or she" personal pronouns. Going to the plural is the best way out. "If people have what they need, they are satisfied," neatly avoids the more cumbersome, "If a person has what he or she needs, he or she is satisfied." But be sure to keep the plural form constant and don't make the mistakes made by the writer of a courtesy clerk manual:

> The average *customer* spends about $40.00 per week in our stores buying groceries to feed *their* family.
> Change the way you thank *each customer* to make it personal to *them*.

Using the plural "their" and "them" keeps away from the wordy "his or her" but is incorrect when used with a singular subject, "the average customer" and "each customer," or a singular object "family." Only two choices are available: for correct usage, either make the subjects plural or the pronouns singular.

> *Average customers* spend about $40.00 per week in our stores buying groceries to feed *their families*.

Or:

> The average *customer spends* about $40.00 per week in our stores buying groceries to feed *his* or *her family*.

Since the point of the second example is individual attention, using a plural "them" would not work. For the right meaning and to correct the grammar, revise to:

> *Change the way you thank each customer* to make it personal to *each one*.

B. *Pronouns as subjects or objects*. Otherwise well-educated people can goof up on this one, particularly when using compound subjects or objects. As an example, fill in the blanks with "I" or "me":

> Despite the storm, the roads are safe for you and
> ____.
> Despite the storm, the roads are safe for you and
> ____ to drive.

In the first sentence, "me" is correct because "you and me" is the object of the preposition "for." In the second example, "I" is correct because it is the subject of "to drive." Follow me?

If you are in doubt about the correct pronoun, take each word that means a person and use it separately in the sentence. Suppose you want to write that your district manager took you and your colleague to a meeting and you don't know which of the following is correct:

> George Maxwell took *he* and *I* to the meeting.
> George Maxwell took *him* and *me* to the meeting.

To find out which is right, use the device of dealing with the pronouns one at a time:

> George Maxwell took *him* to the meeting.
> George Maxwell took *me* to the meeting.

You can tell by the sound that George wouldn't take "he" to the meeting, therefore "him" is correct, so "me" must be, too.

C. *Dangling, misplaced phrases*. We already identified this problem under "Silly Sentences" but let's look at why we get ourselves into such fixes. Usually, the problem occurs because we mix up *who* is doing *what*.

> In talking with Bob yesterday, he mentioned that the annual report is due.

Here, the writer was so involved in the annual report being due, he or she forgot that it was the *writer* who was talking with Bob, and therefore the *writer* had to be the subject of the next clause.

> In talking with Bob yesterday, *I* learned that the annual report is due.

Here's another one:

> After three years of silence, the reporter said the company president was now ready to talk.

Although it sounds that way, it wasn't the reporter who had been silent for three years.

Suggestion: Whenever you start with a modifying phrase and come to the first comma, stop and ask yourself who or what that opening phrase should be attached to. Then use the subject next so it doesn't get hopelessly separated from the phrase.

D. *Misused adjectives and adverbs*. Do you write "I feel bad" or "I feel badly"? If you have trouble deciding whether to use the *ly* form of the word, ask yourself if the sentence expresses any action. With action, you need *ly*; without action, you don't. "I feel badly" is not correct because emotion rather than action is expressed. Both of the following are correct but have distinctly different meanings:

> I smell bad.
> I smell badly.

Explanation:

> I smell bad (because I ate onions).
> I smell badly (because I have a cold and my nose is
> stopped up).

The second sentence involves the *action* of smelling, whereas no action occurs in the first.

When the sentence has more than one verb, you may not be able to make the same adjective or adverb do double duty.

> Anyone who looks or acts differently will be under
> suspicion.

This is wrong because "looks" calls for an adjective since no action is involved. Correction:

> Anyone who looks *different* or acts *differently* will
> be under suspicion.

Highway signs reading "Drive slow" and "Go slow" have disturbed some persons who are careful with their grammar. But "slow" and "slowly" may both be used to describe how an action is performed. The same goes for "quick" and "quickly." These represent those annoying exceptions to rules that make writing life difficult. When in doubt, consult the dictionary to see if the questioned word is an *adj.* or *adv.* or both.

Four most common spelling mistakes

Any word not spelled phonetically or the way it's pronounced becomes a candidate for the blooper list. Types of words most likely to cause errors are:

A.   Words with unstressed vowels, which are either swallowed or pronounced "uh." Examples: balANCE, sponSOR, indepenDENT, sepARate.

B.   Words with ie or ei, which, despite the famous "i before e, except after c" rhyme, crop up as exceptions. Examples: either, counterfeit, foreign, beige.

C.   Words with similar sounds but different meanings. Examples: principle/principal, altar/alter, weather/whether, its/it's.

D.   Words which may or may not double the final consonant. Examples: refer/referred, benefit/benefited, confer/conferred/conference.

Two indispensable tools for writers who want to improve their grammar and spelling are (1) a desk-size, current dictionary and (2) a little book called *Look It Up*.[2] Flesch's book, *Look It Up*, is quicker and handier than the dictionary because he has anticipated those problem words and phrases that most often trip us up and doesn't bother us with the rest. He not only explains correct usage and spelling but gives suggestions on how to remember them.

If you want to improve your spelling, keep track of the errors called to your attention and the words you need to look up. Keep a running list, in a notebook, of the words you want to master and cross them out only when you are no longer in doubt about them. In studying your list from time to time, concentrate on the *part* of the word that gives you trouble. Do you forget the "u" in "restaurant," for example? Figure out a memory device, such as the sound of "aw" as in "aw, shucks," to remind you that it is "au." Let Let your ear and eye reinforce each other.

Good spellers learn to visualize the word. Accurately picturing the word, in effect imprinting it on the brain, seems to be the most effective way to learn to spell.

Three most common punctuation mistakes

When viewed as the simple act of separating sections of composition so that the meaning may be clear to the reader, punctuation becomes a less difficult feature of writing. Words and sentences that run on without pause confuse the reader and may cause him or her to stop reading entirely. Effective punctuation not only clarifies meaning, it also provides emphasis, tempo, and rhythm.

A. *The comma*. By far the most significant punctuation mark, the comma separates and organizes sentences in vital ways. Too many commas, on the other hand, interrupt meaning.

Too few commas: The world it seemed to him once was his oyster, but later he discovered as many before him had that the oyster was inedible and contained no pearls.

Too many commas: It was a bright, sunny day, when John, walking beside his father, saw, crawling, on the sidewalk, a green caterpillar, with the wooliest back, he had ever seen.

Use commas only within a sentence and for the following major purposes:

1. To separate long independent clauses in a compound sentence. Example: The manager has not answered the customer's letter, and I doubt that he ever will.

2. To separate a long phrase or clause from the following independent clause. Example: When he finished misting the fresh vegetables and straightening the rows, he went upstairs to the office.

3. To set off parenthetical phrases. Example: Bobbie asked about the special assignment given her, it seems, because she missed that part of the meeting.

4. To divide elements of a series. Example: The ad featured sale items from the detergent, dog food, cereal, and baked goods categories.

5. To separate two adjectives each of which modifies the noun separately. Example: I noticed the district office report was printed on buff-colored, expensive paper.

When in doubt about the need for a comma, read the

material out loud. If you find yourself pausing for clarification, chances are good you need a comma or some other punctuation at that point.

B. *The semicolon:* Semicolons have fewer uses than commas, but perform virtually the same function. At the risk of over-simplification, let's just say that semicolons are stronger marks than commas and signify a greater break or pause between sentence elements that are of equal weight. Use semicolons to separate two or more parts of a sentence, one of which (at least) is somewhat complex. Separating the two parts into different sentences is one way, but if the parts seem to belong together, then a semicolon works best.

No need for a semicolon: She walked rapidly along, evidently unaware that she was being followed.

Needs semicolon: She walked rapidly along, bemused and deep in thought; evidently she did not know she was being followed.

The semicolon, like the comma, can be used with or without a conjunction. Examples: Someone once said that in most contracts, the large print giveth; the small print taketh away. Writing a good business letter takes effort; however, the results can be very rewarding. Semicolons should not be substituted for colons, which signal that a series or list follows, nor should they be used to introduce, enclose, or end a sentence.

C. *The apostrophe.* In many ways the apostrophe seems to be disappearing like the Dodo Bird. Maybe because they fear using the apostrophe incorrectly, writers get into the subconscious habit of leaving it out. Apostrophes, however, can be very useful as marks of omission ("mornin'"), to indicate a contraction ("isn't that so?"), to form the possessive ("Cynthia's hat"), and to form coined plurals ("The x's equal the y's.").

But where do you put the troublesome thing when the word

ends in "s" or even "ss"? Here again, the book *Look It Up* is a lifesaver. In five paragraphs on page 22, Flesch gives you almost all possible situations in which to use the apostrophe correctly with proper names, singular and plural.

A last piece of advice here, relating to grammar, spelling, and punctuation: don't slow down your writing each time you come to an uncertain spot. Postpone the puzzlement and the looking up until the editing phase. Just make certain that mistakes don't slip through to the final version.

Making Language Work for You

Now let's leave the problems and pitfalls and summarize this section by outlining what writers can do to come out winners in the language struggle.

1. Work at being clear and specific.

The responsibility for the employee's understanding of any message rests with the manager as communicator. Merely knowing what you want to say is no guarantee of clarity. Writing and rewriting, always with the reader in mind, get rid of ambiguities and distracting mistakes.

2. Work at being interesting and colorful.

Words not only mean, they also suggest. Airlines used to flash signs that said, "Hook up your safety belt." Something about that word, "safety," scared people. Now the signs read "Please fasten your seat belt." Consider also the difference between "illegal alien" and "undocumented worker."

The better your vocabulary, the more color you can insert in your writing. But I'm not recommending you learn a lot of big, impressive words. Gather up more unusual words—unusual not

in the sense of obscurity, but that they seldom get used.
Some samples:

bamboozle
bumptious
claptrap
flabbergasted
frugal
hubbub
jampacked
jocular
liven
maverick
meager
motley
murky
romp
serendipity
skinflint
smarmy
smidgen
spangle
zippy

3. Work for a style that has force and conviction.

For readers to pay attention and take intelligent action, they must believe in what was written. Scrupulous accuracy, total truth, and sincerity add up to conviction. Readers can usually detect whether the writer seems to believe, and is willing to stand behind, what he or she has written. Are facts presented in a forthright or obscure manner? Does the material demonstrate correctness of style and form? Is the purpose clear? Short sentences have more force than long ones. Forceful writing grabs attention, builds to a climax, and doesn't leave the reader wondering how the writer stands.

4. Work to be brief.

A lean, barebones style helps both the writer and reader. Readers can handle only so much before they reach the absorption limit. With experience, you can learn to say just enough and then quit.

Summary

Language must be viewed from the perspective of what it will mean to the reader. Language-centered problems to solve include (1) writing that is vague or ambiguous, (2) an old-fashioned or overblown style, (3) misused words, and (4) sentences in which the logic is faulty or the references get misplaced. The most common pitfalls in grammar, spelling, and punctuation can be jumped over or sidestepped with practice. Language is most effective when writers work at being clear and specific, brief, interesting, and colorful, and if they develop a style that has force and conviction.

Notes

[1]The abstraction ladder concept was developed by S. I. Hayakawa. For further information, see S. I. Hayakawa, *Language in Thought and Action*, 2nd ed. (New York: Harcourt, Brace and Company, 1964). See also Louis E. Glorfeld, *A Short Unit on General Semantics* (Beverly Hills, Calif.: Glencoe Press, 1969).

[2]Rudolf Flesch, *Look It Up: A Deskbook of American Spelling and Style* (New York: Harper & Row, Publishers, 1977).

8

EDITING FOR READABILITY

Will you help me make it through to the end?

Professional writers regard their first drafts as raw material and operate on the assumption that editing and rewriting will always be necessary to shore up any first, primitive effort. This attitude frees writers from worrying about high quality the first time around; they just put the ideas down as quickly as they come, using double or triple space to facilitate later editing. For the second or third version, however, standards must get higher and higher, which often means large chunks will get cut out or radically changed. Good writing is more distilled than devised.

It "smarts" when you have to decide that clever turn of phrase doesn't add to the sense or the flow and, therefore, must go. But pain eases at the sight of a well-rounded, yet economically lean, paragraph or page. Sentences that are neat and sure, as well as accurate and clear, more often result from rewriting than from writing.

You edit to make the material more readable. But what is readability? If the reader finds your writing interesting and understandable, you have achieved readability. The subject matter, the selection and arrangement of words, sentences and paragraphs, and even blocks of type, contribute to readability.

Some language experts, however, have worked out an additional meaning. To them, readability has to do with the *ease* of reading and the notion that if readers encounter simplified symbols, of the type they prefer, they will be more receptive. In this framework, short words and sentences add up to readability, while long words and complex sentences, along with unnecessary words or ideas, do not. Material written for graduate students will not appeal to fifth graders, *but not necessarily vice versa*.

Principal proponents of this view of readability have been Rudolf Flesch, who developed a Readability Formula, and Robert Gunning, who worked out a Fog Index. [1] Both systems are based on analyzing writing samples of at least one hundred words in order to count the average numbers of syllables, words, and sentences. Writers who put their material to these tests can determine if their writing tends to be clear (say no more than 15 words per average sentence and no more than 150 syllables per average 100 words), or relatively murky or even obscure at higher counts.

Such schemes are valuable, particularly if the writer already has an inkling he or she writes over people's heads or puts them to sleep with nonstop sentences or padded paragraphs. Yet one weakness in applying mathematical formulas to determine readability is that, except for newspaper and magazine authors, most of us do not write for a generalized readership. You tailor managerial writing for specific readers and purposes. At least to some degree, you must assume shared understanding of issues and problems. Reducing the number of syllables, words, or sentences won't make the material more readable for the reader who lacks the basic subject or professional background to understand.

Another weakness of such formulas rests in their arbitrary scales and classifications. For instance, I put the first 200 words of this chapter in its rough, first-draft stage through several analyses. (Since I don't plan to rework the figures for later drafts, what you are now reading may not jibe exactly.) According to a formula, roughly adapted from the work of Flesch, Gunning, and Smith, it came out like this:

	Total words	Average words per sentence
First four sentences	107	26.7
Next four sentences	50	12.5
Average for both samples		19.6

The first sample would get bad marks, coming out somewhere between *hazy* and *cloudy,* whereas the second sample gets A+ for being *very clear.* Combining both samples, the average words per sentence improves greatly but would still be categorized as not quite "clear."

As I wrote those first eight sentences, I was trying for clear meaning and paying no conscious attention to word or sentence length. I was also trying for variety of pace, which may account for the significant difference in sentence length between the first four and next four sentences.

Now let's look at syllables.

	Number of Syllables	Classification
First 100 words	140	Clear
Next 100 words	162	On the border between clear and misty
Average for both samples	151	Clear

The second group of four sentences had *fewer* words but *more* syllables. Come again? Sure, that often happens. The second sample included words like "economically" (six syllables), "understandable" (five syllables) and "readability" (five syllables). Most readability formulas would call these all "big" bad words.

But they are not *difficult* words, being well within the experience of the average reader.

Rather than worrying about formulas, then, let's just agree that long and rambling material tires anyone. But the solution won't be found in short, choppy sentences. Our overall goal is to develop a clear, strong writing style, regardless of numbers of words or syllables. The editing process provides our best tool.

The Editing Process

When you look at what you have just written, and reach for a pen or pencil, you have begun the editing process. For complex material, such as reports, the procedure usually goes something like this:

First, you put aside your first draft for a "cooling off" period. Try to forget about it for a day or two so that when you pick it up again, you scrutinize it with a fresh, more critical eye.

Second, you skim the whole report, not from your perspective but from the prospective reader's viewpoint. Try to imagine a reader who lacks your background in the subject and is coming to the material "cold." What will your writing mean to such a reader? Does it hang together? Are the general purpose and the main ideas clear? If the answer to one or more of these questions is "No," then you have identified your first editing chore.

Third, after correcting the major problems uncovered so far, you read the material again, but this time you go slowly and carefully. No skimming. At this stage, you look for specific problems to solve. More about this later.

Fourth, you continue reading and revising until you either feel satisfied or run out of time. (Some of us are *never* satisfied and have to let deadlines force a halt.)

Procedurally, editors usually draw lines through matter to be deleted, make small corrections between the typed or written lines or in the margin, and indicate additions by arrows or insert marks (ʌ), putting longer additions on separate pages.

When even the writer has trouble reading it, the manuscript

must either be retyped or rewritten for the person who will do the final processing. (I prefer to retype my own material during all the preliminary drafts because I notice more problems while I retype and I edit better with a typewriter than with a pencil.) Other essential editing tools are scissors and tape and/or staples. If, for example, you have a fairly unmarked paragraph that needs to be moved, cutting and rearranging save time over retyping or rewriting.

Fifth, you prepare for the final version. Does it *look* interesting? If not, should you chop some of the paragraphs into smaller segments with additional subheadings? Refer back to Chapter 2 for the section on the role general appearance plays. Make all the necessary decisions about final format, method of reproducing and distributing.

Sixth, say goodbye to the report and heave a sigh of relief.

To help illustrate the typical process of editing, here is a sample paragraph from another book I am working on.

Original draft

To help bolster your confidence, especially during the initial stages of the negotiation when your fears will be the greatest, you can develop a good lead-in that can be used in many of your negotiations. This will enable you to get by the most difficult part which is usually the start. Professional athletes, no matter how much experience they have, will tell you that they are nervous and tense until the game starts. Once the action begins, their nervousness and tenseness leaves them and they are free to concentrate on the business at hand.

First revision

To help bolster your confidence, especially during the

initial stages of the negotiation when your fears will be

the greatest, you can develop a good lead-in ^to get you past that-can-be

the difficult starting point.
used-in-many-of-your-negotiations. This-will-enable-you-to

get-by-the-most-difficult-part-which-is-usually-the-start.

Professional athletes^ and performers of all kinds, no matter how much experience they

have, will tell you that they are nervous and tense until

the game^ or performance starts. Once the action begins, however, ^their nervousness

and tenseness ~~leaves-them~~ disappear and they are free to concentrate

on the business at hand.

Second revision

To help bolster your confidence, especially during the

initial stages of the negotiation when your fears^ are apt to will be

the greatest, you can^ learn to develop a good lead-in to get you

past the difficult starting point. Professional athletes

and performers of all kinds, no matter how ~~much-experience~~ experienced,

~~they-have~~, will tell you that they are nervous and tense

until the game or performance starts. Once the action

begins, however, nervousness and tenseness disappear and

they are free to concentrate on the business at hand.

108

Notice that the editing process not only improves the writing but also provides the opportunity to introduce new and better concepts that were not a part of the original draft and did not occur to the writer until the editing was under way.

Problems Your Editing Needs to Solve

As promised, let's now identify some problems that call for editing. They come in three varieties: (1) editing for clarity and readability; (2) editing for mistakes in grammar, spelling, or punctuation; and (3) editing to polish and improve the style.

1. Editing for clarity and readability

Chapter 7 discussed language usage that caused unclear writing. In your material, do you find words or phrases that are vague, ambiguous, or equivocal? Has jargon been overworked? Do some terms reside on the top rungs of the abstraction ladder? Do your facts, figures, and other data add to or detract from understanding? Be honest, now. Above all, keep the reader's welfare in mind when trying to decide whether your writing is sufficiently clear.

Your editing may also reveal that your unclear writing came from unclear or incomplete *thinking*. So much better that *you* discover such flaws while they are correctable, rather than confound your readers.

2. Editing for mistakes in grammar, spelling, or punctuation

You were advised in the last chapter not to slow down the first draft because of uncertainties about grammar, spelling, or punctuation. Now you need to be concerned about them. Use as your guide the most common errors identified in Chapter 7.

If you edit for meaning *to the reader,* you will be more apt to notice that one of your parenthetical phrases needs commas at both ends, not because of a rule but to *make sense.* With the reader in mind, you watch for those silly sentences or misplaced phrases, like "Slamming the door behind her, the interview was over."

A good general rule is, when in doubt, look it up. Also try reading the questionable passage out loud. Does it sound funny? If so, editing is a must.

3. Editing to polish and improve the style

Although by no means an exhaustive list, the following six aspects provide a beginning check list for what to work for when editing to polish:

A. Conciseness, concreteness. When managers look at the stacks of paper on their desks, they may suspect that brevity, like the miniskirt, has gone out of style. It appears as if some business writers expect to be paid by the word.

On the contrary, brevity is still not only the soul of wit, it is also the catcher and holder of attention. Conciseness goes a step beyond brevity. Keeping the material as short as possible, such as a telegram, may not contribute to good communication if the result is dull or obscure. Conciseness, on the other hand, aims at writing that gets its point across in the fewest possible words, but without losing clarity, tone, or interest.

Allen Weiss said it well:

> Business writing should be economical, with every word carrying its own weight. *Every word must contribute to conveying a message, clarifying a point, or enhancing readability.*[2]

Editing for conciseness and concreteness means reducing fat prose and deleting pretentious terms. A particular target of your editing should be those overly long, maybe even tortuous circumlocutions, those wordy sentences full of redundancies that seem to go on and on, ending where we cannot guess, meandering quite a bit like this one. Still there? Although repetition and restatement enhance meaning and emphasis, your editing should ruthlessly delete those sections in which you overstate or overwrite. If you don't strike oil in the first two paragraphs, stop boring.

B. Viewpoint. As advised earlier, managers should write more from the *you* than the *I* or *they* perspective. All three perspectives have merit, of course, but your editing checks to see that your selections have been wise in relation to your audience and purpose. In business writing, a self-centered, look-at-me viewpoint is less effective than a you-the-reader approach. For more formal writing, however, all kinds of personal pronouns should be minimized or avoided entirely.

Too frequent shifting back and forth among viewpoints can confuse and discourage the reader. Edit so that shifts occur only when dictated by logic or for a needed change of pace.

C. Active voice. Bear down on your verbs and adverbs. Make them vigorous and alive because the verb propels the sentence. Rewrite sentences like, "It was decided that important changes would be made." Not only is the verb passive ("it was decided") but the sentence fails to explain who decided.

Closely inspect all forms of the verb "to be." Can more active verbs replace "is," "are," "was," or "were"? Neither the passive voice nor the various forms of "to be" can or should be eliminated entirely; they serve important functions. But overuse of these inert forms produces dull and lifeless writing.

D. Color, rhythm, variety. As a direct reflection of the writer's person and personality, style cannot be taught or adequately described.[3] We recognize a given writer's style but would be foolish to try to copy it. We must develop our own. In your editing, however, you can look for an *absence* of style. Perhaps your writing appears clear and error-free but somehow lacking in zip. You can now edit to add some life and flair.

Color results when vivid words replace ordinary ones. Searching for that single "right" word takes time and effort but rewards both writer and reader. Mark Twain noted that the difference between the right adjective and the next-best adjective is the difference between lightning and lightning bug. Also consider the difference one letter makes in the two words, belonging and belongings.

Get a good dictionary with simple synonyms and antonyms. Specialized dictionaries, or the classic volume, *Roget's International Thesaurus*, are probably too complex for general business use. But I recommend them for people who delight in words and language.

Rhythm comes from the pace of words, sentences, and paragraphs. Some writers develop a rhythm that moves the reader comfortably along with both force and variety; others seem to bog down. As a rule, long sentences retard the pace while short sentences create a sense of movement and urgency. When appropriate, arrange details in increasing strength or importance, building to a climax. Start strong, finish strong, and put less important material in the middle.

Variety calls for a change of style and pace. Watch that your sentences are not monotonously alike in length or arrangement, or begin and end with the same kinds of words or phrases. Try inverting the order of sentence elements. Mix up short and long sentences. Don't vary the writing just for the effect but in order to hold attention and clarify meaning. Too much variety, which makes the material sound affected and unnatural, may be worse than none at all.

E. Consistency. Just as the manager needs consistent messages coming from her or his office, so should the manager's style display balance and consistency. Working to achieve overall and internal consistency in a report means that you will check on how ideas are held together and make sure they maintain balance and form. You will watch for such aspects as the following:

Consistent maintenance of acceptable usage	Does part of the report use slang, while other parts do not?
Handling of jargon	Are jargon terms defined in some places but not others?

Shifting viewpoints	Do you unnecessarily move from "he" to "you" to "they"?
Spelling of names or concepts	Are the same versions used throughout?

Even individual sentences need consistency. For example, can you spot why the following is out of whack?

> He was encouraged to sign up for training by the wishes of his wife, the advice of his teacher, and to justify his boss's faith in him.

This sentence lacks parallel form because the series of phrases, all similar in form, should complete the preposition "by," and the last one does not. To restore consistency, rewrite to:

> He was encouraged to sign up for training by the wishes of his wife, the advice of his teacher, and the faith his boss had in him.

Can you write with consistency and variety, too? Yes. Try for variety of pace but consistency of form.

F. Reader direction. While editing your material, make sure you have carefully led the reader through all parts of your communication. Does your report quickly give the reader a frame of reference and an overview of what's ahead? Does each element of the message display a close link to those elements that came before and those that follow? Do key ideas stand out from subordinate ones?

Readers need help to understand the *relationships* between concepts, paragraphs, and sentences. Merely passing from one idea to the next confuses the reader; you need to show what connection idea two has with idea one and tie the two together. We sometimes use punctuation to provide transition (as with the semicolon in the previous sentence). Another method is to number or label points to show similar categories. But your intended meaning comes through mostly with the help of transition and connective words and phrases.

As one way to tell if you need transitions, check the beginning word in each paragraph and the first word of each sentence within a paragraph. Is that word usually "the," or some other word you have unconsciously used repeatedly? Pass the transitions, please.

Commonly used transitions are "although," "however," "because," and "moreover." Each has a different meaning and therefore a different purpose. Work to expand your transitions and get away from the overuse of "but" and "and."

When you can't think of an appropriate transition or when you want a change from the standbys, consult the following list. Note that the function of the connective comes first, which means you have to decide what you want the transition to do before you can choose the best one.

Transition Words and Phrases

1. **Temporal, Time:** previously, formerly, at an earlier period, at the same time, in the same period, throughout this period, during this time, meanwhile, in the meantime, then, by that time, already, now, since then, after this, thereafter, in the end, at last, at length, at a later time, now that . . .
2. **Demonstrative:** thereof, thereby, therein, therefrom, in this case (respect, etc.), in such a case, at such time, on such occasions, under these circumstances, here, in all this, in connection with this, here again, together with this . . .
3. **Marking Reference:** in point of, with respect to, as related to, concerning, as for . . .
4. **Summarizing:** to sum up, to recapitulate, to review, to abstract the main points, in summary, in conclusion, on the whole, briefly, in a word, in short, as we have seen, up to this point, in other words . . .
5. **Concluding:** to conclude, in conclusion, finally, last, last of all, to wrap up, to bring to a close, to end . . .

6. **Citing:** for instance, for example, to illustrate, by way of illustration, another case (example), a case in point . . .
7. **Excepting:** with this exception, except for this, leaving this out, excluded, excepted, exclusive of, irrespective of . . .
8. **Marking a Change in Tone or in Point of View:** in another sense, at least, seriously, to speak frankly, for my part, in fact, to come to the point, in general, of course, you see, as the matter stands, as things are, but, however, on the other hand . . .
9. **Comparative:** parallel with, allied to, comparable to, from another point of view, in the same category, in like manner, in the same way, similarly, likewise, yet, even, still, more important, of less importance, next in importance, in contrast, conversely . . .
10. **Emphatic:** indeed, moreover, what's more, add to this, furthermore, besides, further, even without this, in addition to this, all the more, even, yet, especially, in particular, how much more, yet again, above all, best of all, most of all . . .
11. **Inferential:** so, therefore, consequently, accordingly, thus, hence, then, in consequence, as a result, the result is, we conclude (infer), in this way, because of this, for this reason, this being true, such being the case, under these circumstances, it follows from this that . . .
12. **Casual:** this is because, this is to be explained by, the reason is, the explanation is to be found in, why? . . .
13. **Concessive:** certainly, indeed, it is true, to be sure, it must be granted (conceded), I admit (confess), true, granted, admitting, no doubt . . .
14. **Adversative:** yet, still, nevertheless, however, on the other hand, at the same time, nonetheless, only, even so, in spite of this, after all, in all events . . .
15. **Refuting:** otherwise, else, were this not so, on the contrary, no, never, hardly . . .
16. **Connectives-of-All-Work:** first (second, etc.), in the first place (second, etc.), the former, the latter, in general, in particular, to continue, to return, to repeat, to resume, along with, as I have said, farther on, then, now, again, once more,

further, too, also, in fact, at any rate, at all events, as it is, incidentally, parenthetically, by the way, as follows, namely . . .

17. **Correlative:** on the one hand ____, on the other ____; in the first place ____, in the second place ____; whereas ____, therefore ____; as long as ____, so long as ____; if (while, though) ____, yet ____; wherever ____, there ____; just as ____, so ____; if ____, also ____ (all the more, how much more); since ____, then ____; the more ____, the more ____; not only ____, but also ____ .

The Special Problems of Editing Other People's Writing

Since objectivity about one's own writing is hard to come by, having other people do the editing provides a potential solution. In business writing, however, this process both helps and hinders. When several managers write separate parts of a report, a disinterested person could successfully edit for consistency of style and insert transitions to link up the parts.

On the other hand, the supervisor who insists on editing all the material written by his or her subordinates trains them to dash off material any old way because they believe it will be changed no matter how well they write it. Unclear authority lines may cause some managers to consistently edit their subordinates' writing. If the original writer was not sure who was to do what, the writing obviously suffers. How many levels of review must the writing pass? What is the scope of the manager's role as editor? To suggest revisions for the writer to carry out? To critique? To do the actual editing? Confusion about writing and editorial discretion fouls up the best of writing efforts.

Jurisdictions for both writing and editing assignments therefore need clarification. Written communication flow and responsibility should not be left to chance.

Editing other people's work, moreover, requires you to tread lightly and tactfully. When you criticize someone's writing, that person may have difficulty accepting criticism as "constructive," because you are hitting that person right in the ego. Pride in authorship exists in us all.

If a cooperative spirit exists between writer and editor, the subordinate will profit from editing suggestions and eventually become a better writer. Better writers make better employees. So handle the editing of other's writing with care and with awareness of the consequences beyond the written material.

The Proofreading Process

Final manuscript preparation will be easier if some proofreading has been done at each stage of preparation. But now thoroughly check for completeness and accuracy as the last item of business before having the material reproduced. Standard proofreading symbols can be found in any dictionary and are well known to most typists.

Effective proofreading requires you to abandon your normal reading speed and virtually examine each word and punctuation mark separately. This time through, don't read for meaning but to find mistakes and typing errors. Accuracy improves, particularly on longer, more complex material, if the proofreading is done by a team. One person reads aloud from the manuscript, while another follows from the original copy. This process more quickly spots such problems as accidentally omitted matter, items out of order, or incorrect figures. One person trying to compare two copies at once soon gets a headache.

Summary

The essence of readability boils down to whether the reader wants to read what you have written and understands what you mean. Editing and rewriting often take longer than writing but make all the difference in the end product's quality. Editing improves clarity and readability, and weeds out mistakes in grammar, spelling, and punctuation. In addition, the editing process polishes and punches up your writing style. (Editing other people's material can be a trickier problem than editing your own.) Before final reproduction, the proofreading process calls for word-by-word scrutiny for errors.

Notes

[1] Rudolf Flesch, *How to Test Readability* (New York: Harper & Row, Publishers, Inc., 1951); and Robert Gunning, *How to Take the Fog out of Writing* (Chicago: Dartnell Press, 1964). See also: Terry C. Smith, *How to Write Better and Faster* (New York: Thomas Y. Crowell, 1965).

[2] Allen Weiss, *Write What You Mean: A Handbook of Business Communication* (New York: AMACOM, A Division of American Management Associations, 1977), p. 121.

[3] One little 85-page volume comes as close as possible: William Strunk, Jr., and E. B. White, *The Elements of Style*, 3rd ed. (New York: The Macmillan Company, 1979).

9

REPORT WRITING

Who, what, when, where, why, how—and so what?

Everything discussed in this book so far applies to report writing. Managers must go through the same processes (planning, gathering information, assembling, interpreting, organizing, writing, and editing) as for other kinds of writing. So what makes a report worth special attention?

Whether formal or informal, routine or special, reports have significance as essential management tools. Managers use reports as instruments of control, to detect defects or problems in organization structure and functioning, and, above all, as the basis for decision-making. Reports measure performance against planning, control costs, provide reference and documentation, and coordinate activities of scattered segments of an organization.

Usually longer and more complex than other written communications, reports take up large blocks of managerial and staff time. Their bulk and scope make them more difficult than memos and correspondence.

Writers who routinely grind out reports may forget the *purpose* of the report is to answer a question or solve a problem. Regardless of whether the question has been asked by someone else (the district manager wants to know the loss rate on shopping carts) or by the store manager (how are we doing compared to last year?) the report's function is to provide the answer. As communications to customers, employees, or upper management, reports focus on facts and new information; you find out the facts and then come back and tell what they mean.

Another aspect that sets reports apart involves the slow feedback response; word comes back even more slowly than for other forms of written communication. Reports take longer to research, write, reproduce, and distribute, as well as to read and respond to. Budgets and other constraints may prevent reports from being acted on quickly. Report writers, therefore, must keep potential delay in mind. What effect will elapsed time have on the data included, the words chosen, and even the mailing list?

Kinds of Reports

Conceding the possibility of overlap, business reports are usually designed for either *external* or *internal* use, on either a *regular* (monthly, annual) or *irregular* basis. Typical external reports would be those required by government agencies like Federal Drug Administration (FDA), Occupational Safety and Health Administration (OSHA), and Equal Employment Opportunity Commission (EEOC). The agencies usually supply forms on which to put the required numbers and other information. Since little leeway exists for narrative explanation or originality within the closely prescribed format and procedure, your main job is to provide accurate, clear, and timely information.

Internal reports at the managerial level generally fall into the following kinds:

1. Administrative

When prepared by managers themselves and/or their subordinates, administrative reports help achieve control in such areas as in the giving of directions, the firm's financial status, and the supervising and disciplining of employees. Often, administrative reports are handled on preprinted forms so that the problem for the manager is how to fit all relevant details into limited space.

Samples: Sales records; performance activities of units, divisions; periodic budgets and audits; personnel records, evaluations; grievance and accident reports; returned merchandise; damaged goods; and losses from fire, burglaries, equipment use, or chemicals.

2. Planning, problem-solving

Short-term and long-term reports in this category identify anticipated problems and make projections of needs and future accomplishments. Both recurring problems and the unexpected may be the subject of planning and problem-solving reports.

Samples: Budget requests and justifications; personnel needs; personnel turnover studies; projections of training needs and program designs; formulating company goals and objectives; requests for talks, tours, or participation in community activities; adverse news reports; and consumer boycotts or demonstrations.

3. Research

The most highly developed type of special business report, the research report provides answers to people in authority, answers vital to decision-making. Almost all data gathered can be labeled "research," but here it means the non-routine "let's find out" kind of report.

Samples: Market analyses; organizational efficiency studies;

analysis of facilities design, use, and effectiveness; opinion surveys; comparative cost studies; policy changes; and effects or implications of shoplifting or bad checks.

Importance of the Reader

Before deciding whether and how to write a report, you need once again to consider your potential readers. Do they need the information? Will they use it? Will they read the report conscientiously or skim?

Levels of interest and need vary among report readers. Why labor over details that go unread?

To find out what their managers wanted in reports, a large manufacturing corporation did extensive surveys and came up with some startling responses. Their managers reported that they all (100%) read report *summaries* but that was the only section so well read. About 60 percent read the *introduction*, and slightly more than 50 percent read the *conclusions*. Now get this. Less than 25 percent read the *body* and only 15 percent read the *appendix*.

When busy managers read report summaries, they wanted to know right up front what the report was about, including its significance and implications, and the action called for. If the managers saw the report summary as relevant, they may then go on to read the introduction and body. Reasons given for reading more than the summary were if they were (1) specially interested in the subject, (2) deeply involved in some aspect of the project, (3) sure the problem was urgent, or (4) skeptical of the report's conclusions. Report readers didn't like to have to hunt for the answers to such questions as what should be done, how much it will cost, and what courses of action are available.

The significance of these findings for report writers looms large. Technical and detailed matter must be written in terms of the reader and his or her projected use of the material. Most readers want only the essence, not the details. Put key back-up information in the appendix and save the rest for those few who will ask for it.

Typical Report Formats

Formats differ widely from a one-page tabulation of requested figures to a complex combination of research results and project proposals running hundreds of pages. Several matters may dictate format styles and lengths: company policy, time available, the prospective readers, and what response or action the writer wants.

The process of report writing contains one important step that other business writing may not. Before writing can begin and intelligent decisions about format made, the report writer must be in consultation with other people in the organization to get agreement on objectives, clarification of purposes, and a clear understanding of why the report is needed. If you skip this step, you will turn out reports nobody wants or reads.

Organize short reports in ways similar to these:

Introduction	Brief pre-summary
Findings	Introduction
Discussion	Body
Details	Conclusions
	Recommendations

Include all or most of the following in longer, more formal reports:

Cover. Protective binders are customarily used, with or without printing or other identification.

Title page. Don't use vague or literary sounding titles. "The Cutting Edge" may wax philosophical but fails to indicate what the report is about. Clearly state the subject, the origin of the report, the organization or unit for which it was prepared, and other identifications. The title page should also include the name or names of the author(s) in alphabetical order or according to seniority or rank. List only those who did the work, not those with high status or who authorized the project or assisted in minor ways.

Letters of authorization, acceptance, transmittal, approval. Depending upon company policy, letters may or may not accompany and/or be a part of the report.

Prefatory material. A preface or foreword can explain why the report was written and give appropriate acknowledgments.

Table of contents. A topical outline of the major and minor sections, along with their page numbers.

Introduction. Use as a separate section delineating objectives and purpose or omit if introductory material has been included elsewhere.

Summary of findings. A summary of information or conclusions, often in the form of an *abstract*, which can be either *descriptive* (a short overview to help the reader decide whether to read the entire report) or *informative* (summarizes the main points and gives the principal data and conclusions).

Body or discussion. Gives detailed answers to the questions raised in the introduction and provides links between the factual data and the writer's conclusions. Describes and discusses the whole picture: description of the problem, its history, definition of terms, methods used, equipment required, presentation of data and other information, such as what was done and how.

Conclusions and recommendations. Explanation of the scope, importance, and significance of the findings and proposed next steps.

Appendix. Pertinent information, such as test results, that need not be read earlier in order to understand or use the report. Footnotes and references should appear here unless they have been put at the bottom of pages.

Exhibits. Tabulations, drawings, photographs, or sample materials not used in earlier sections because they are too detailed or too specialized for the average reader.

Bibliography. Listing of books, periodicals, and other documents used in the report and which the reader would find useful for further background.

Index. Necessary only for very long reports and if the Table of Contents does not break down into minor sections. Whereas the Table of Contents was a chronological listing of report sections, the Index is an alphabetical arrangement of concepts and subject matter with corresponding page numbers.

Summary

In many ways similar to other kinds of business writing, report writing presents additional problems because of length, complexity, and delayed feedback. Reports are prepared for either external or internal use and appear on a regular or irregular basis. Internal managerial reports function primarily for administrative, planning, or research purposes. Report formats vary from simple to complex, depending on the purpose and the needs of the reader and situation.

Summary

10

CHOOSING AMONG MEDIA

How come the medium really is the message?

Managers cannot function without the giving and getting of information. Employees who know where they fit in the organization and why their work is important, and especially those who feel appreciated and "in on things," are obviously better employees who derive greater satisfaction from their work. Failure of the company to tell its story leaves the way open for misinformation and demoralizing rumors. Without adequate facts and background information, decision-making and problem-solving suffer.

In the process of management, how is the word passed along (up, down, and across) the echelons and out to the public? Managers usually have favorite methods. Some are "memo happy," while others rely heavily on bulletin boards, staff meetings, and reports.

Favorite media may get to be favorites, unfortunately, not because of their favorable impact on readership but because of habit or tradition, or because they are quick and easy media *for the manager.* This chapter will identify strengths and weaknesses for a variety of media, as well as criteria for their selection. Although oral forms such as meetings, interviews, and telephone conversations occupy a large share of managerial time and attention, our discussion will naturally focus on the visual media. As you know, written communication often extends or confirms personal contact.

Multiple media are widely used in business because of multiple purposes and readership and because using more than one channel buys more insurance that important messages will get through. Sometimes, however, a single medium will do the job and more than that would represent information overload. How can you tell which media work best for which message? Consult the following chart (pages 130-137), which analyzes 17 types of media used by managers for both internal and external communication, and the subsequent section on criteria, to find out.

Criteria for Media Selection

Readers seldom notice or think about the medium through which the message arrives. When they receive a good letter they aren't conscious of the medium and are aware only of the message. Employees may not know or care that the manager went through a complicated process to decide (1) which method would work best for which purpose; (2) whether to transmit a single message or wage a campaign of concurrent and/or sequential messages; and (3) whether to use one medium or a combination. But effective managers are always very much aware of the relative merits of the spectrum of media, and continually check them against the following factors:

1. Complexity

Does the problem involve more than a few people, levels, or units? What is the scope and what are the ramifications of the situation? Will the reader see the significance quickly or will detailed explanations be necessary?

2. Importance

Importance to the communicator, the company, and the reader must be weighed. What seems vital to the manager may be of only passing interest to the intended reader, and, of course, the other way around. Managers should ask themselves first what the reader already knows, needs to know and wants to know, and in lower priority, what the managers want to tell. Will the message affect paramount issues like profit and loss or the financial wellbeing of the company? Will it deal directly or indirectly with the work or personal life of the employee?

3. Urgency

What are the time factors involved? What is the differential between the time available and the time it will take to communicate the message? What are the costs of delay?

4. Desired response or purpose

Will the message provide general information or call for specific action? Is the purpose behind the message a change in attitude, opinion, or behavior?

5. Readership, message receivers

How many potential readers are there? Do they represent a variety of levels, interests, attitudes? Are they scattered geographically?

MEDIA ANALYSIS

Media	Strengths
Advertisements	Newspaper and magazine insertions sell goods, services, foster public relations. Convenient; reach wide audience at relatively low cost. Useful to take stand on public issues.
Announcements, instructions	Useful as reference sources about company and its policies and procedures. Available in permanent form. Somewhat useful for employee orientation and training.
Articles, news releases	Build, maintain, prestige via trade journals, association presses, as well as local publication. New products, processes can be announced, discussed at little cost. Good source of shop talk exchange. Reprints can be shared with wider audience.
Attitude surveys	Means of learning what employees and customers think and want. Also includes message that management cares about opinions. Can cover many subjects, areas.

MEDIA ANALYSIS

Weaknesses	Comments
Usually routine, impersonal. Space and function limitations. Reach only self-selected readers.	Except for product listings, should supplement rather than replace other communication media.
May not be generalizable to more than one group of employees. Managers may not want some policies publicized. Over a period of time, mass of instructions may add up to red tape and reduce managers' initiative.	Most suitable for important messages affecting entire organization or of interest to large numbers of people.
Require news slant, careful planning, preparation. Best written or ghost written by professionals. May have long time lag before publication so not effective for timely or urgent messages. May not get published or read.	Difficult to measure impact on readership.
Polls difficult to design, administer, analyze. May not get honest, objective information. Small return may not represent true cross section.	People who respond are usually very much for or against something.

Media	Strengths
Brochures, pamphlets, circulars	Flexibility of subjects. Convenient to distribute. May be mailed, used as "stuffer," or displayed.
Bulletin boards, chalkboards, flip charts	Convenient, inexpensive, highly flexible. Easily changed. Especially suited for brief, timely news.
Displays, exhibits, information racks	Can quickly tell a story, introduce new product or explain a service. Useful means to display casual, changing material on broad subjects, and make items available to be picked up. High attention value.
Form letters, direct mail pieces	Flexible, can reach many people with same message quickly, less expensively than individual letters. Modern technology making mass mailings appear more personalized.
Letters	Familiar medium that can be both informative and provide documentation. Can go to one person or many. Easy to use, relatively inexpensive. Can reach people at a distance. Can be personalized for high impact.

Weaknesses	Comments
Require skill in writing, layout, artwork. Because of "throw away" attribute, may be expensive in terms of short life.	Most effective when professionally produced and used as supplement to other media.
Limited space. No control over who reads. Require regular cleaning, servicing. Not useful for long messages.	Eye appeal and strategic placement essential.
Reading and selection of material voluntary; no control over who reads or takes material. Erecting, servicing, dismantling required.	Eye appeal and strategic placement essential.
Require mailing list maintence as well as mass production capability.	Canned message has negative impact when trying to masquerade as personal letter.
May encourage time lag. Require filing methods and equipment.	Universally accepted and widely used medium.

Media	Strengths
Manuals, handbooks	Simplify instructions, save time and trouble. Explain tested procedures. Provide constant reference. Useful for indoctrination.
Memos, bulletins	Flexible, quickly produced and distributed. Provide documentation, permanent record and act as reminders. Convey or request information. Establish or confirm policy, authority. Informal format (From the desk of So and So) or more formal (To/From/Date/Subject/Purpose).
Newsletters, house organs	Present company positions, policies in newsy, informal format. Can reach many readers quickly. Flexible, convenient, inexpensive, and can be somewhat personalized. Can also serve ombudsman function.
Orders, other forms	Blank spaces for fill-ins save words, time. Useful shortcuts for regular and repetitive activities that need documentation, standardization.
Posters, signs	Attention-getting. Easy to understand. Useful for spot announcements and occasional reminders.

Weaknesses	Comments
Difficult and costly to prepare. Need constant revisions. Hard to make both comprehensive and readable.	Commonly used medium to inform and educate, especially new employees.
Tend to be "dashed off" and overworked. Require filing methods and equipment. Unless skillfully planned and organized, can reflect inconsistencies and contradictions in policy.	Backbone of documentation process. Work best if limited to single point or theme.
Demand reporting and writing skill, as well as adequate budget to make attractive. May be conflict between news format and employee personal or gossip features.	Depending on level and skill of staff, such publications can be effective means of communicating important messages in behind-the-scenes mode to employees and their families.
Tend to be dull, regimented. Cannot be personalized. May discourage initiative.	Can expedite procedures like accounting. May be taken for granted so new employees not properly trained in use and do not understand ramifications.
Limited to single, simple themes. Require artistic skill or professional execution. Require continual replacement.	Eye appeal and strategic placement essential. Effective as part of information campaign.

Media	Strengths
Reports	Provide in-depth information, problem identification, solution, and permanent record. Evaluate progress, efficiency. Useful for decision-making.
Rules, policy statements	Clarify company mission, specific procedures such as purchasing, accounting. Provide reference, especially for new employees. Work best when explaining what should *not* be done.
Suggestion systems Customer:	When customer complaints or suggestions are communicated directly to the employee or unit involved, work becomes more important and relationship between work and customer satisfaction understood. Clarifies unit or store standards.
Employee:	Provides opportunities for upward communication, ways to improve policies, procedures. Encourages creativity, high morale. Works best if anonymity protected, where desired, and rewards are given for improved systems or efficiency. Can vary from Suggestion Box to columns in company publication.

Weaknesses	Comments
Require skills of analysis, organization, writing. Take time, effort. Tend to be too long, involved, encouraging scanning rather than reading.	Essential to management control.
Difficult to initiate, amend, or get approved. Compilation and organization require skill, effort, filing methods and equipment. Difficult to distinguish between ordinary memo and policy announcement.	Useful if well organized, regularly updated, and if made conveniently available to all employees.
Require methods, forms, personnel. Difficult to solicit on regular basis and present in coherent, organized way. Difficult to distinguish between one dissatisfied customer and public at large.	Perhaps only effective means to measure public pulse.
Hard to convince employees that suggestions sincerely wanted and will be acted upon. Planning, methods, and personnel required. Needs constant promotion, reminders, and follow-up.	System can include other media such as forms, reports, newsletters. Best administered by committee.

BEST MEDIA FOR EACH CRITERION

Criterion	Internal Communication (inside the store or chain)	External Communication (outside the store or chain to the public)
Complex messages	Letters Manuals, handbooks Newsletters Reports Rules, policy statements	Articles, news releases Letters Newsletters Reports
Important messages	Announcements Bulletin boards Displays, exhibits Letters Memos, bulletins Newsletters Reports	Advertisements Articles, news releases Brochures Letters
Urgent messages	Announcements Bulletin boards Displays, exhibits Form letters Letters Memos, bulletins Posters, signs	Advertisements Letters
Desired response: To *inform*	Announcements Form letters Letters Manuals, handbooks Memos, bulletins Newsletters Orders, forms	Advertisements Brochures Form letters Letters

Choosing Among Media

Criterion	Internal	External
To *get* *information* or *action*	Announcements Attitude surveys Letters Memos, bulletins Suggestion systems	Advertisements Attitude surveys Form letters Letters Suggestion systems
To *persuade*	Letters Memos, bulletins Posters	Advertisements Letters
To *win* *friends*	Attitude surveys Letters Memos, bulletins Newsletters Suggestion systems	Articles, news releases Attitude surveys Form letters Letters Newsletters Suggestion systems
Readership: *Few*	Letters Memos, bulletins Reports	Letters
Many	Form letters Manuals, handbooks Newsletters Orders, forms Rules, policy statements	Advertisements Brochures Form letters Newsletters
Scattered	Announcements Brochures Form letters Manuals, handbooks Newsletters	Advertisements Articles, news releases Brochures Form letters Newsletters

Criterion	Internal	External
Interest:		
High	Announcements	Letters
	Bulletin boards	Newsletters
	Displays, exhibits	
	Letters	
	Memos, bulletins	
	Newsletters	
	Posters	
Low	Letters	Advertisements
	Memos, bulletins	Brochures
	Newsletters	Letters
Cost:		
High	Brochures	Advertisements
	Letters	Brochures
	Manuals, handbooks	Letters
	Reports	Reports
	Rules, policy statements	
Low	Announcements	Articles, news releases
	Bulletin boards	Form letters
	Displays, exhibits	Orders, forms
	Form letters	
	Memos, bulletins	
	Orders, forms	
	Posters	
Circulation:		
Direct	Announcements	(Not applicable)
	Brochures	
	Letters	
	Memos, bulletins	
Many layers	Bulletin boards	(Not applicable)
	Displays, exhibits	
	Manuals, handbooks	
	Newsletters	
	Posters	

6. Interest value to the reader

Will the message touch on the personal self-interest or work life of the reader or will the message be viewed as only peripherally relevant? Will attention levels be high or low? Will the reader be able to see at once what is "in it for him" or will he or she have to dig through many details to find out?

7. Cost

Does the value of the message justify elaborate formats, fancy covers, and expensive artwork? Will sufficient attention be paid to a less attractive, low-budget approach? What are the relative costs and benefits from a mass mailing format contrasted with specially prepared, personalized letters?

8. Circulation

Who will get the information when? How much of the information is apt to be filtered or distorted as it goes through layers and channels? Should each reader get a copy or can supervisory personnel be relied upon to spread the word, and spread it accurately? What would happen if a key person is on vacation and the word doesn't get around when it should?

You may disagree with my assessments on pages 138-140 of the "best" media to use in relation to the criteria because your needs and experience have dictated different choices. That's fine. My list was intended as a starting point and general guide only. Just to show how preferences can vary, let's see what other managers prefer.

When managers from a variety of businesses and industries reported on the effectiveness of visual media in their internal and external communication, this is how they ranked the media they used:[1]

Considered most effective (top ranked)	Considered least effective (bottom ranked)
Exhibits, displays	Posters
Company publications	Information racks
Advertisements	Trade journals
Handbooks, manuals	Mail surveys
Orders, forms	Reports

The Media Are Messages, Too

Message forms and formats have a way of becoming messages in themselves. How you choose to present your communication may carry more weight than the ideas conveyed. Regardless of the words used, the quality of paper and the professional appearance of the brochure speak volumes about the company.

Remember also that media can indirectly (but powerfully) influence policy. An established, long-standing personnel manual, for example, may cause people to create subsequent material to *fit the manual* and reject new policies requiring extensive manual revision. What's more, it may become the practice to slip in even crucial personnel policy changes through routine revisions of the manual rather than by announcing them.

Summary

The effective selection of media deserves more attention than it usually gets. The shape, direction, and timing of a communication may either enhance or counteract all the effort you have put into the content and organization. You can make better selections if you understand each medium's strengths and weaknesses and the basic criteria upon which to make choices. Each medium choice can be a message in itself.

Note

[1]Reported in Robert D. Breth, *Dynamic Management Communications* (Reading, Mass.: Addison-Wesley Publishing Company, 1969), p. 211.

APPENDIX

DISCUSSION QUESTIONS, EXERCISES, AND CASE STUDIES

CHAPTER 1: WRITTEN COMMUNICATION

Discussion questions:

1. Review the definitions of communication on page 1. Can you improve them?
2. Why is communication considered a process? What aspects make it dynamic?
3. In what ways can writers try to improve the quality of feedback they get?

Exercises:

1. Select a subject about which you may be asked to write a report. Indicate your topic and what you believe your main idea will be.

2. Identify the number of people who are apt to read the report. Who are they?
3. List the sources from which you could get the necessary information for your report.

Case Study:

Assistant Manager Mike posts a notice on the bulletin board, announcing that the strike against a major cereal manufacturer is continuing and asking that customers be told why some cereals are temporarily out of stock. Mike includes in his notice the request that grocery clerk, Cory, make an explanatory sign for the cereal section.

Just before going off duty, Mike sees that no sign has been made and summons Cory.

"Where's the sign I asked for?" he asks.

"What sign?" is the clerk's response.

"Don't you ever check the bulletin board?" Mike snaps.

"I checked it about two o'clock and didn't see anything that applied to me," Cory answers.

Mike thinks back and realizes he posted the notice about 2:15 P.M. It is now almost 4:30.

What was the cause of the problem? What might the assistant manager do to prevent similar problems from occurring in the future?

CHAPTER 2: ATTENTION

Discussion questions:

1. What are your favorite openings and closings in business letters? Why?

2. In what ways do business-letter writers let the reader know the letter's purpose?
3. How do the following relate to attention?
   spacing
   neatness
   accuracy
   letterhead
   margins
   subheads

Exercises:

1. Think of the last two business letters you read. Identify those qualities that caught and held your attention.
2. List as many ways as you can think of to show the reader how your letter relates to him or her.
3. Evaluate the following letter for its attention-getting effectiveness:

> TO: ALL STORES AND RETAIL
>   DIRECTORS
> FROM: TOD SIMPSON
> SUBJECT: HOLIDAY SCHEDULING

> *REMINDER*
> THE WEEK OF NOVEMBER 20TH IS A HOLIDAY
> WEEK . . . .
> WATCH YOUR SCHEDULING.
> ANYONE SCHEDULED *O V E R* THIRTY-TWO
> HOURS IS ON OVERTIME.
> THIS SHOULD BE PERSONALLY CHECKED BY
> EACH MANAGER TO INSURE WE DON'T OVER-
> SCHEDULE.
> THANK YOU.
>   TOD SIMPSON

Case Study:

A district manager plans to write a letter to all meat department and store managers about the upcoming meat department inventories. He wants to counteract problems encountered during the last inventory when standard methods were not used. He wants to stress the following:
1. All meat departments should take inventory on the same Sunday morning.
2. Supplies of meat should not be lowered because of the inventory.
3. Meat managers should report results promptly, including how long the process took and how many personnel were involved.

What advice would you give to make the letter get and hold attention? How would you write the letter?

CHAPTER 3: PERSONALIZATION

Discussion questions:

1. What qualities does it take to make effective use of humor in business writing?
2. How do you feel about the use of "Dear So and So" in business letters?
3. Do you like to use first names in business correspondence? Why?

Exercises:

1. Rewrite the following to make better use of personal pronouns:
    It is of concern for Ruth and myself to get the project done right and sent to the manager quickly. Will be interested in response from he and you.

2. Rewrite the following to shift emphasis from "we" to "you":

> We have been trying to reach you to discuss an incorrect billing. We feel an error has been made and we are anxious to straighten out our accounts. We would appreciate a prompt response.

3. Select a subject for a business report, then choose an audience you already know. Now consult the list of Audience Analysis Needs on page 28 and put down as much information as you can about your potential readers. Where are the gaps? Can you write a successful report without filling in the gaps?

Case Study:

Store Manager Ray is pleased with how all personnel pitched in to achieve record sales over the Fourth of July weekend. He doesn't have time to thank each one and has decided to put his compliments in a letter, and send a copy to the district office.

What can Ray do to personalize the letter, even though it will be sent to more than thirty people?

CHAPTER 4: PURPOSE

Discussion questions:

1. Why should we be able to separate our motives and purposes in business writing?
2. What can and should you do when you can't figure out the letter writer's purpose?
3. Which do you prefer to receive: letters with the purpose identified at the top or in the text? Why?

Exercises:

1. Which of the following are purposes and which are motives?

   try for a promotion
   impress the reader with your knowledge
   convince the staff to work harder
   look good on paper
   explain a new policy

2. List three circumstances under which you would need to write a letter *to persuade*.

3. Identify the writer's purpose in the following letter:

To:	All Unit Managers
From:	Don Smith, Manager
Date:	April 1, 1980
Subject:	Summer vacations

   Spring is here and so is the time to get summer vacations nailed down. As you know, vacations cause us difficult scheduling problems every year, what with trying to give every permanent, full-time employee his or her first or second choice and having to pull in temporary help to cover.

   Please work out your preferred unit schedule and give it to me no later than April 15. I will coordinate all schedules and get back to you with confirmation or changes by May 1.

   Remember: I must have your schedules *no later than April 15*. Otherwise, you and your staff will have to take what's left.

Case Study:

Study the following letter and answer the questions posed.

Dear Mr. Store Manager:

What kind of a place are you running anyway? Yesterday at 11 a.m., right in the middle of your store, I was afraid for my life!

Another shopper and I arrived at the check-out stand at the same time and we both were in a hurry. She deliberately rammed her cart into mine. I rammed hers back.

Your checkers and baggers just stood there and watched while that woman forced her way into the line ahead of me, shaking her fist under my nose. Was that fair?

Lillian Walker
(A very disturbed cus-
tomer who may go find
another store to trade in.)

What are the writer's possible purpose and motives? What is the response she is apparently hoping to get from the reader?

CHAPTER 5: GATHERING INFORMATION

Discussion questions:

1. Why should inferences not be confused with facts?
2. When you read a report, how can you tell the difference between facts, opinions, inferences, and judgments?
3. What are the relative merits of check-off versus open-ended questions in opinion polls?

Exercises:

1. List the main sources of information you use when you must write a report.

2. Design a questionnaire that could be used for an employee opinion poll on attitudes about a fringe benefit such as paid holidays, vacation, pensions, or insurance.
3. Pretest your questionnaire on some friends and colleagues in order to discover any problems in it.

Case Study:

Store Manager Ted has been asked by his superior to conduct an Organization Survey to determine how all personnel feel about their jobs and the firm. Upper-management people want to be able to gauge how policies and practices contribute to satisfaction or dissatisfaction, and collect data for dialogue, problem-solving, and action. Ted's survey will be a pilot study which may later be expanded and used throughout the chain.

What suggestions would you give Ted about the information he needs, and where and how he can find it?

CHAPTER 6: ORGANIZATION AND STRUCTURE

Discussion questions:

1. What are the benefits of organizing before you start to write?
2. What are the goals of organization?
3. Which of the organization patterns (described on pages 64-66) are easiest to use? Why?

Exercises:

1. Find a carbon copy of a letter you have written and check it against the five characteristics of style (on page 62). Do you see aspects in need of improvement?

2. What organization pattern or patterns did you use?
3. What kinds of supporting material did you use?

Case Study:

Assistant Store Manager Joan has asked your help in organizing a bulletin she needs to write to all store personnel on how to improve price-change procedures. She has compiled the following ideas:
1. Our store and the whole chain will benefit if the process of handling price changes can be improved and lost revenue is regained.
2. We need to figure out where the system breaks down.
3. All unit managers should begin to work on this problem tomorrow.
4. The staff should respond more quickly to price changes.
5. We lose money every time a clerk is slow in changing prices on the products.
6. When the store loses money, you lose money.
7. The store loses money when there is a time lag between the receipt of new prices and getting them stamped or written on the products.
8. There seems to be unnecessary delay because of confusion about responsibility.
9. One thing to do right away is analyze how price changes are handled now.
10. The correct procedure is spelled out in the manual; your job is to see that it is implemented.
11. You need to retrain or reorient your staff in the correct procedure.
12. Some of the staff are apparently confused about the priorities among their job functions.

To help her outline her material effectively, point out:
1. The purpose statement
2. The thesis statement

3. The organization pattern you think will be most effective
4. The major topic sentences

CHAPTER 7: LANGUAGE AND MEANING

Discussion questions:

1. What are some of your "pet hates" in language usage?
2. How do you react when you see grammar or spelling errors in business writing?
3. In what ways do excessive, unnecessary words impede communication?

Exercises:

1. Mark the following sentences as (1) okay, (2) overblown, or (3) old-fashioned.

> In spite of the fact that there may be an economic slow-down, it is understandable that your highly respected firm is exceedingly anxious to secure the services of competent employees who more and more frequently have undergone specialized and detailed training.
>
> Will you have a management trainee opening in your firm next year?
>
> Pursuant to your request, enclosed herewith is the aforementioned application to which I respectfully directly your attention.
>
> You have a vacancy in your accounting department and I am prepared to fill it.
>
> It is my earnest conviction that in your search for promising prospects you will proceed eventually to the eminent college from which I am about to graduate.

2. Rewrite the following to eliminate the "indefinite it" and passive verbs:

> Upon checking at the store it was found that it is not easy for trucks to back up to the loading dock.
>
> It was requested by Eloise that the space be left clear.
>
> Since I feel there is confusion and conflict still remaining from the reorganization, let us immediately put it to rest.

3. Rewrite the following to improve the problem of misplaced phrases:

> One day coming home from work about mid-March, the air was permeated with the rich, sweet smell of newly turned earth.
>
> To understand the report, it must be read carefully.
>
> Inspecting from the front to the back of the store, many safety violations were found.

Case Study:

You have received the following copy of a letter written by one of your subordinates:

> My Dear Mrs. Pearson:
>
> I have just received your letter about the problems you encountered in our store.
>
> Gee, you got me on this one. Our store personnel have great reputations for making customers happy. So I have to say, we have got to work on this. Yes, see if we can get your problem resolved.
>
> Thanks for writing and letting us know you had these problems. Now we have the opportunity to get you back in our store again.
>
> Best regards,
> Rob Foster

As Rob's boss, you decide he needs some feedback and criticism on his use of language. What would you do and say?

CHAPTER 8: EDITING FOR READABILITY

Discussion questions:

1. What is the most difficult aspect of editing? Why?
2. What is the role of style in business writing?
3. In what ways can you improve the way you edit your own writing?

Exercises:

1. Analyze a sample of your writing to determine the average number of words and syllables in a sentence. What have you learned?
2. Edit the following material. See if you can find at least seven mistakes.

Rapid changes are taking place in our industry. These changes require you to have better education and training, however, very few courses have been developed which are closely related to the management and operation of a supermarket. How can we persue improvement even though it is evident to all that few opportunities are available to you and I.

One exception to this is the home study program developed by Cornell University, which worked with experts in the food industry and other fields to bring us valuable information to increase your knowledge and improve your skills.

3. List the factors in the previous paragraphs which required editing for polishing or improved style.

Case Study:

Study the following edited material, then answer the questions.

~~The purpose of~~ this brief report ~~is to bring you up to~~ `will tell you how`

~~date on the status of~~ the new personnel survey. ~~It is my~~ `is going, and will also make`

~~intention to make a recommendation to you in relation to the~~ `some recommendations to help you`

~~course of action you can possibly pursue in making your decision~~ `decide what to do`

about several personal matters. For example, we face a critical

shortage of high-talent management trainees. ~~In fact, it has~~ `Moreover,`

~~been suggested by the majority of~~ current business indicators `most`

~~that the typical employee today must increase their profi-~~ `suggest`

~~ciencies~~ and knowledge ~~on a continuing basis~~ merely to keep up `skills` `continually`

with the changing times.

157

1. How effective was the editing?
2. Were any mistakes in usage, grammar, spelling, or punctuation overlooked?
3. Do you see other ways to improve the writing?

CHAPTER 9: REPORT WRITING

Discussion questions:

1. Why are reports considered essential management tools?
2. What are some ways you can speed up the receipt of feedback on your next report?
3. What part of a long report do you read first? Why?

Exercises:

1. Organize the following material into a report outline:

    Body or discussion
    Summary of findings
    Letter of transmittal
    Recommendations
    Report abstract
    Preface
    Acknowledgments
    Description of problem
    Bibliography

2. Identify the following as either administrative, problem-solving or research reports (or possibly a combination):

    Employee performance appraisal
    Survey of customer shopping patterns

Courtesy clerk training program
Projected personnel needs during summer vacations

3. List some things you can do to improve the readership of your next report.

Case Study:

Sally's Soopers Chain is expanding so rapidly the company size will double within five years. Because of increasing geographical dispersion, top management plans on eventual total decentralization of decision-making to the local store manager. But some managers are having problems learning to run a decentralized store.

Previous management training programs consisted of rotating a trainee through the various store departments. Growth pressures, however, call for a totally new approach with the capability of producing large numbers of managers trained in many new skills in short periods.

The problem has been handed to the Corporate Training Department, which plans to propose a programmed instruction approach which managers can work on as part of their regular assignments. The course will consist of learning activities and specific abilities the trainee must demonstrate to his or her own as well as the supervisor's satisfaction.

You have been put on special assignment to help with planning, analysis, and report writing. Training modules will be a part of the report.

1. State the problem as you understand it.
2. Identify the potential readership.
3. Decide where information might be gathered.
4. Pick a tentative organization pattern.
5. What do you anticipate will be the most difficult aspect of turning out this report? Why?

CHAPTER 10: CHOOSING AMONG MEDIA

Discussion questions:

1. Of the 17 kinds of media analyzed on pages 130-137, which is your favorite and why?
2. If the message is important but not urgent, which medium or media would you choose for internal communication if you have a low budget? Why?
3. Why do you suppose the companies surveyed about media effectiveness (pages 141-142) ranked exhibits high and reports low?

Exercises:

1. Evaluate the relative merits of brochures, form letters, and newsletters to tell the company's story. Justify your analysis.
2. Identify those company policies which should be communicated in ways *other* than in official Rules and Policies Statements. Explain your answer.
3. List some subjects that could best be communicated by posters placed in strategic locations in a food store. Would your answer be different for messages directed to the public as well as to employees?

Case Study:

Store Manager Walter has a series of promotions, transfers, and resignations to announce. Discussing the changes in staff meetings last time didn't get the message across to all employees. The next newsletter won't be published for three weeks.

What would you recommend Walter use as his first choice of media to communicate in this situation? Second choice? What factors most influenced your recommendations?